The Genesis 'Gap Theory'

The Genesis 'Gap Theory'

Its Credibility and Consequences

by

M. W. J. Phelan, B.Th., M.Th., Th.D., Ph.D.

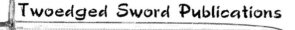

Twoedged Sword Publications

The word of God is sharper than any twoedged sword, piercing even
to the dividing asunder of soul and spirit. (Hebrews 4:12)

The right of M. W. J. Phelan to be identified as the author of
this work has been asserted in accordance with the Copyright,
Designs and Patents Act 1988.

© European Theological Seminary
And College Of The Bible 2005

First published 2005

ISBN-13:   978-1-905447-02-2

ISBN-10:   1-905447-02-7

Twoedged Sword Publications
PO Box 266, Waterlooville, PO7 5ZT
www.twoedgedswordpublications.co.uk

Acknowledgement

This study was written originally as a part of my course work for the degree of Doctor of Theology with The European Theological Seminary And College Of The Bible. Because of this the copyright belongs to the Seminary. I would like to thank the Honorary President, Professor Gordon Beck, and the rest of the Academic Faculty for allowing it to be published by Twoedged Sword Publications.

I am particularly grateful to the Chancellor of the Seminary, Professor Raphael Gasson, who is a first-rate Hebrew scholar, and who kindly read the text before publication to confirm my statements concerning Hebrew Grammar. He also offered some helpful suggestions concerning presentation. It was an honour for me that such an excellent scholar was prepared to review my work.

I would also like to show my appreciation of Paul Rose of Twoedged Sword Publications, for the useful and very practical suggestions he made which have brought several improvements to this study. I wish also to thank my good friend John Morris, who first suggested I examine the subject.

Finally, I would like to thank my wife, Joy Marion, whose endless and generous patience and good-humour allowed me to undertake the task of preparing this work for publication.

The European Theological Seminary And College Of The Bible

The European Theological Seminary And College Of The Bible is an international and non-denominational accredited Seminary that stands unequivocally for the literal truth of the Scriptures of the Old and New Testaments, and is firmly opposed to both Modernism and Liberalism.

The seminary offers a very wide range of courses, from Certificates and Diplomas to Doctorates. Evidence Of Prior Learning is warmly welcomed, and the seminary is able to offer its students the benefits and convenience of Distance Learning and Continuous Assessment.

The Honorary President would welcome applications for enrolment with the seminary by readers of this book, and will do all he can to accept them as suitable candidates for *European Theological Seminary And College Of The Bible* scholarships.

Please write for a free Prospectus to;

Professor G. S. Beck, (Dept. TES/GGT)
170 Shore Road,
Greenisland,
Carrickfergus,
County Antrim, BT38-8TT.

Contents

Introduction

The interpretation of Genesis 1:1–2 has taxed the minds of exegetes for many years. The controversy has centred upon whether or not there is a chronological gap of unspecified duration within the compass of what, at first glance, seems to be continuous narrative. This proposed gap is the basis of what might be termed theories-of-accommodation. By some the proposed gap is used to accommodate the alleged vast ages of cosmic, geological, and biological evolution, and has certain similarities with the theory that views the days of Genesis 1, not as literal days representing but one complete rotation of the earth upon its axis, but as entire epochs, during which the earth was subject to profound, but extremely slow evolutionary change. This is a view frequently advocated by so-called Theistic-Evolutionists, who seek to harmonise Scripture with human wisdom in the form of evolutionary dogma.

The facts are that;

1) the six days of Genesis 1 are each defined as comprising but one 'evening and morning' (verses 5, 8, 13, 19, 23, and 31),

2) Exodus 20:11 and 31:17 state that the basis of the seven-day week which regulates our calendar still, is the hexameron, or six days of creation followed by the Sabbath rest,

3) death did not exist before Adam, and came through Adam (Romans 5:12), ruling out the possibility of millions of years of plant and animal deaths before man, and,

4) the concept of the history of the events of Genesis 1, being greater in duration than all the rest of Scripture history taken together, and of it outlasting it by a

truly prodigious amount which the adoption of an
evolutionary time-scale would demand, is absolutely
contrary to the conceptual basis of the Word-of-God.

The desire to accommodate entire epochs such as are
suggested by evolutionists within a chronological gap to be
located within Genesis 1:1–2 then should not be a serious
consideration for sincere students of the Word.

But the proposed gap is used also to accommodate the Luciferic
Rebellion and Fall. It is taught by believers in this view that the
original creation was marred, if not ruined altogether by this
rebellion, or by a Divine Judgement which fell upon the earth as
a consequence of it, and that the hexameron details the actions
of God in restoring the, by then, ruined earth. Such a view is
best represented by Arthur Custance in his *Without Form And
Void*,[1] a work produced with the help of my first instructor in
the Scriptures, Mr. A. G. Tilney, former Honorary Secretary of
The Evolution Protest Movement. It was this scholarly work
which, some time ago, led me to believe that there was a sound
Scriptural basis for the Gap Theory. Whenever I refer to the
Gap Theory within this monograph, it is to be understood in this
second aspect, namely that of providing accommodation for a
pre-Adamic Luciferic Fall.

Finally, there are those who see such a gap accommodating
both evolutionary epochs, and the Luciferic Rebellion, such as
G. H. Pember, in his well-known, *Earth's Earliest Ages*,[2] a
work which inspired Custance.

What the sincere student of God's Word needs to know is;
whether or not there is any real basis in the Scriptures

---

[1] Custance, Arthur C., *Without Form And Void*, Brookville, Canada,
published privately by the author, 1970.

[2] Pember, G. H., *Earth's Earliest Ages*, London, Pickering & Inglis,
undated.

themselves for the existence of such a gap, or whether the proposal is based only upon human speculation. It is my aim to address this question in this small volume.

In Part One, I examine the text of Genesis 1:1–2, and discuss the view that there is a gap before Genesis 1:1, as well as the more usual theory concerning a gap between Genesis 1:1 and 1:2. In Part Two I examine certain other Scriptures which are used by Gap Theorists to support their views, while in Part Three I explain the consequences of accepting the Gap Theory. Part Four contains four appendices and a bibliography.

Inevitably, as proponents of the Gap Theory claim to derive much support from the grammar of Genesis 1:1–2, this book discusses many technical matters. To assist the reader, I give below an Hebrew–English interlinear representation of Genesis 1:1–2a using the Masoretic Text. Hebrew is read from right to left. The English translation is that of the Authorized Version. The words in bold text are those that are dealt with in detail in the study.

Verse 1.

הארץ	ואת	השמים	את	אלהים	ברא	בראשית
the earth.	ואת = 1 + ה 1 = and	the heaven	*untranslated indicator of the direct object*	God	created	In (the) beginning

Verse 2a.

תהום	על -פני	וחשך	ובהו	תהו	היתה	והארץ
the deep.	was upon the face of	and darkness	and void	without form	was	And the earth

11

Part One

Is there evidence of a gap
from the text of Genesis 1:1–2?

Chapter One

Is there a gap before Genesis 1:1?

In attempting to decide whether or not there is a chronological gap within Genesis 1:1–2 there are very many points to consider. We begin with a detailed examination of the key words of Genesis 1:1. In the Authorized Version, this text reads as follows,

> "In the beginning God created the heaven and the earth."

The first three words of this translation, "In the beginning," are a rendering of only one word in the Hebrew text; the word bereshith, בראשית. The second word of the Hebrew text is not *God*, the word following "beginning" in the Authorized Version, but bara, ברא, the word translated as *created* (see the interlinear text on page 11).

Part A: בראשית

The Relationship of Genesis 1:1, to 1:2, and 1:3

The first consideration relates to these first two Hebrew words of Genesis 1:1; *bereshith*, בראשית, and *bara*, ברא, and, which using the Authorized Version translation would be rendered, *In the beginning created*. It is suggested by some that their form indicates that the creation they refer to is one imposed upon a pre-existing formless and unfilled earth which is referred to in verse 2. This suggestion then supposes that a gap, or unspecified period of time is to be located *before* Genesis 1:1. The normal view for Gap Theorists, is that the gap occurs between verses 1 and 2. It is a surprise to many, including some 'normal' Gap Theorists, that there is more than one position for the placement of the alleged gap. The strength of and widespread support for the argument referred to above are both often under-estimated. This view results in verses 1–2 being translated along the lines of,

> "In the beginning of God's creating, the earth was without form and void,"[3]

or, omitting the article,

> "In beginning created God the heaven and the earth, and the earth was wastes and voids."[4]

If this view is correct, the alleged period of time prior to verse 2 is *unmentioned* in verse 1. Of course, this would mean that it would be impossible to make any statement about what might, or might not have occurred prior to verse 2. It would appear to be beyond the scope of direct revelation. There might have been a rebellion by Lucifer and subsequent ruination of the earth; there might not. Perhaps it might be said that it would be *unlikely* that any significant action occurred during this proposed age without our being told about it, but any statement at all would be nothing but speculation, and we would have no right to assume we have been told more than we need to know.

---

[3] This is the translation offered by the renowned Hebraist, Norman Henry Snaith, in, *Notes On The Hebrew Text Of Genesis I–VIII*, London, The Epworth Press, 1947, p. 7.

[4] This is the translation found in *The Hebrew Students Manual*, London, Samuel Bagster, undated, in.loc.

The belief referred to above is based upon the syntax of Genesis 1:1. *Bereshith*, בראשית, is formed by the union of the inseparable preposition *beth*, ב, (*in*), and the noun *reshith*, ראשית (*beginning*). A fact that is not often realised is that *bereshith*, בראשית has no article corresponding to the English *the* found in most English versions,[5] which is why *The Concordant Version* names Genesis, *In A Beginning*, (again using an article of course, but making the article indefinite).[6]

A Construct, or an Absolute?

Now *reshith*, ראשית, here, may be understood in two fundamentally different ways. It may be understood either as what is known by Hebrew students as 1) an *Absolute*, or 2) as a *Construct*. I explain the two options below.

1) If *bereshith*, בראשית, is in the Absolute State, and, *bara*, ברא, is a finite verb, then undoubtedly Genesis 1:1 is what is called an Independent Statement declaring that God created the heavens and the earth, and it is unqualified by verses 2 or 3, that is, it is not *dependent* upon verses 2 or 3. This is the view most people who read the Bible in English translation naturally assume, generally being unacquainted with Hebrew grammar. However, there is another possibility.

---

[5] *The Hebrew Students Manual*, op.cit., p. 90, Green, Samuel, *A Handbook Of Old Testament Hebrew*, London, The Religious Tract Society, 1901, p. 143, Davidson, Benjamin, *The Analytical Hebrew And Chaldee Lexicon*, Grand Rapids, Michigan, U.S.A., undated, in.loc., & Gesenius, H. W. F., *Hebrew Grammar*, edited and enlarged Kautzsch, translated Cowley, Oxford, at The University Press, second edition from the Corrected Sheets, 1966, p. 457.

[6] *Concordant Version Of The Old Testament: The Book Of "Genesis": In A Beginning*, Canyon Country, California, Concordant Publishing Concern, 1978, frontispiece, and p. 41.

2) If *bereshith*, בראשית, is what Hebrew students refer to as a Construct, then Genesis 1:1 is the complete opposite of an Independent Statement; instead it is a Dependent Clause, that is, it is completely *dependent* upon the following statement of verse 2 (or verse 3, if verse 2 is considered to be parenthetic), leading to the translations given above.[7]

What is the Construct State?

In English, if we wish to indicate what is called the Genitive Case, we frequently just add an ' 's ' to the end of a noun. Thus in order to demonstrate that a particular word was spoken by God, we could write, *God's Word*, or, if we did not mind being a little long-winded, we could write instead, *the Word of God*. In Greek, instead of adding an ''s', to the end of the noun for God, we would change the ending of θεος (God) from 'ος', to 'ου', so that the phrase reads *o logos* (the Word) *του θεου* (of (the) God). The 'ου' is what is called the Genitive Case ending for this particular class of Greek noun. In Hebrew, unlike Greek, there are no case endings of nouns, nonetheless a genitive relationship may be *constructed* by combining two nouns. This situation is called by Hebrew students the Construct State. By this technique *man*, and *house*, for example, might be brought together so as to show that the house in question belonged to the man. When this occurs, the first noun is said to *govern* the second noun, being in *construction* with it. The first noun, that is the governing noun, is said to be in the Construct State, while the second noun, that is the governed noun, is said to be in the Absolute

---

[7] Fields, Weston W., *Unformed And Unfilled: A Critique Of The Gap Theory*, Collinsville, Illinois, U.S.A., Burgener Enterprises, pp. 149ff.

State.[8] The first noun in the Construct State sometimes changes its morphology, and therefore its pronunciation may be altered. On those occasions where the morphology or form of the word does not indicate the Construct State, its presence or absence must be deduced from the context. This is the situation with *bereshith*, בראשית, in Genesis 1:1. In the Construct State the two nouns are actually considered to be one word. A noun that is not in the Construct State is in the Absolute State.[9] In our case, Snaith, a follower of the Dependent Clause view regards *reshith*, ראשית, as the Construct, and *the remainder of the verse* as the Absolute, thus forming the rest of the Construct form. This is because he understands clearly that the second word *bara*, ברא, is actually a verb, rather than a noun.[10]

Encouragement for the belief that in Genesis 1:1 we are dealing with a Construct is sometimes found in the fact that nouns in this state never have the article, while nouns in the Absolute State, usually possess it.[11] Now *bereshith*, בראשית, is undoubtedly what is called *anarthrous*, meaning that it does <u>not</u> have the article, which, superficially would indicate that we are indeed dealing with the Construct State here, meaning in turn that Genesis 1:1 is a Dependent Clause, showing that the earth had already existed for an unspecified period of time before Genesis 1:1, but now we find another complication!

References to events related to *time*, when they are found in adverbial forms, (such as clearly we find in Genesis 1:1), do

---

[8] Green, op.cit., pp. 50, 157, & 159, and Kelley Page H., *Biblical Hebrew: An Introductory Grammar*, Grand Rapids, Michigan, Eerdmans, 1992, pp. 58ff.

[9] Fields, op.cit., p. 152.

[10] Op.cit., p. 7.

[11] Green, op.cit., p. 157.

not necessarily *need* to have the article at all![12] This means that *bara*, ברא, may be a finite verb, and *bereshith*, בראשית, may be adverbial, making Genesis 1:1 an Independent Clause after all! It is a fact that very many examples may be given of nouns used in adverbial forms without the article, even though they are in the Absolute State.[13] The lack of the article in *bereshith*, בראשית, does not resolve the matter then. It may still be an Absolute, meaning that Genesis 1:1 may still be viewed as an Independent Statement, which would completely rule out the possibility of any history before Genesis 1:1.

There is yet another consideration however. Although *reshith*, ראשית, occurs fifty-one times in the Scriptures, it is only found with the preposition, *beth*, ב, as *bereshith*, בראשית, on five other occasions, and in each it is indubitably in the Construct State! Interestingly, in two of these other occasions (Jeremiah 26:1, & 27:1), it is the very first word in the verse as it is in Genesis 1:1. There is even a reference in the Masorah Magna of the Hebrew Text pointing out this fact, which is possibly why Jewish exegetes, unlike their Christian counterparts, have often understood the word to be a Construct.[14] The Masoretes obviously regarded its other rare occurrences as worth indicating, and Jewish exegetes would have noticed very readily that *every* other occurrence is undoubtedly a Construct, encouraging them to believe that Genesis 1:1 is also. The Jewish exegetes Ibn Ezra and Rashi were both of this view, although they differed slightly in their exegesis. I list the occurrences and show the usage of *reshith*, ראשית, in Appendix I.

---

[12] Fields, op.cit., p. 153.

[13] Ibid.

[14] Kelley, Page H, Mynatt, Daniel S., and Crawford, Timothy G., *The Masorah Of Biblia Hebraica Stuttgartensia,* Grand Rapids, Michigan, U.S.A, Eerdmans, 1998, p. 8.

Ibn Ezra

Ibn Ezra certainly regarded *bereshith*, בראשית, in Genesis 1:1 as a Construct, and therefore viewed it as a part of a Dependent Clause. He believed the main statement to be contained in verse 2. This would result in a translation along the lines of

> "When God began to create the heaven and the
> earth, the earth was without form and void."

Both E. J. Young and Umberto Cassuto challenge Ibn Ezra on this. Young draws upon Cassuto's assertion that if Ibn Ezra's claim were correct, Genesis 1:2 would be expected to read, *and without form the earth*, ותהי הארץ or, *was the earth*, היתה הארץ. Cassuto made the point that Jeremiah 26:1 reads, *In the beginning of the reign of Jehoiachim… came this word*, בראשית ממלכות יהויקים …היה הדבר הזה, a syntactical arrangement noticeably different from Genesis 1:1–2. Cassuto also invited comparison with the opening words of Hosea. Hosea 1:2 reads *The beginning of the speaking of the Lord by Hosea, and said the Lord to Hosea*, תחלת דבר יהוה בהושע ויאמר יהוה אל הושע. This again differs from Genesis 1:1–2.[15]

---

[15] Young, Edward, J., *Studies In Genesis One*, Philadelphia, U.S.A., Presbyterian And Reformed, 1964, p. 1. Young cites Cassuto, Umberto, *A Commentary On The Book Of Genesis* (in Hebrew), 1953, Part I, p. 10. In the first example ממלכות יהויקים… (*the reign of Jehoiachim…*), is inserted between the noun בראשית and the verbal phrase (*came this word*) היה הדבר הזה. In the second example we see a changed morphology of תחלה (*beginning*) by the replacement of the final letter ה, by ת, to form תחלת. The pointing also changes, see Davidson, op.cit., in.loc.

Rashi

Rashi adopted a different view. While he also thought that verse 1 is a Dependent Clause, he made it dependent on verse 3, making verse 2 a parenthesis. This view produces a translation along the lines of,

> "When God began to create the heavens and the earth—the earth being without form and void, with darkness upon the face of the deep, and the wind of God moving upon the face of the waters—then God said, "Let there be light.""

Discussing this view, E. J. Young again draws upon Cassuto, who maintains that if Rashi's view really were correct, we would expect verse 2 to read *and the earth without form and void*, והארץ תהו ובהו, and the *was, (hayetha)*, היתה, would have been omitted. Young says that Cassuto points out that in I Samuel 3:2ff., "the circumstantial clauses are expressed ועלי שוכב and ושמואל שוכב [*And Samuel lying down*, and, *And Eli lying down*, that is without the verb *was*]."[16] [The words in square brackets are my own.]

Supporters of the Construct State/Dependent Clause view point out that it is well-known that other Semitic languages give examples of the use of nouns in the Construct State occurring before finite verbs.[17] It is interesting to note that a recent English version of the Tanakh made by the Jewish Publication Society seems to follow Rashi, translating Genesis 1:1 as,

> "When God began to create heaven and earth—the earth being unformed and void...",

---

[16] Young, E. J. op.cit., p. 2.

[17] Fields, op.cit., pp. 154–155.

and only in a footnote offers the alternative rendering,

>"In the beginning God created..."[18]

This is strikingly similar to the rendering suggested by George Knight in his *A Christian Theology Of The Old Testament*, which offers,

>"When, in the beginning, God created the heaven and the earth, the earth was without form and void..."[19]

Driver also supports a similar translation, citing Dillmann and Rashi,[20] as does the much respected Snaith who, as we have seen, also views *bereshith*, בראשות, as a Construct. Finally, Nahum Sarna in the Jewish Publication Society's commentary on Genesis also advocates this translation.[21]

Robert Young

Robert Young, the compiler of the famous concordance, translates Genesis 1:1a as,

>"In the beginning of"

and observes,

---

[18] *Tanakh: A New Translation Of The Holy Scriptures According To The Traditional Hebrew Text,* Philadelphia, U.S.A., The Jewish Publication Society, 1985, in.loc. A philosophical defence of Rashi's translation by Levenson, Jon. D., is to be found in *The Jewish Study Bible*, Oxford, Oxford University Press, 2004, in.loc.

[19] Knight, George A. F., *A Christian Theology Of The Old Testament*, London, SCM Press, revised edition, 1964, p. 99.

[20] Driver, S. R., *The Book Of Genesis*, London, Methuen & Co., 1905, p. 3.

[21] Sarna, Nahum M., *The JPS Torah Commentary: Genesis*, Philadelphia, U.S.A., The Jewish Publication Society, 5749 (1989), in.loc.

"The Hebrew word thus rendered occurs *fifty-one* times in the Old Testament. In *forty-five* of these, it occurs in the *construct state*, being followed by a noun or pronoun. The remaining instances are Le. 2.12, De. 33.21, Ne. 12.44, (in all of which it appears to be a technical name-first-fruits, i.e. of the land, &c.); Pr. 4.7, '*the first thing* is wisdom;' Is. 46.10, 'declaring the end from *the beginning*.' This last is the only passage in the Old Testament in which the word is used *absolutely* in reference to *time*, and whether it is sufficient to overrule the *forty-five*, is much more than doubtful. Accordingly, the ancient Jewish commentator Rashi, as well as the modern German critics, Bunsen, Ewald, &c., have preferred understanding the next Hebrew word [*bara*, ברא,] as a noun, not as a verb. Viewed in this light the passage reads thus: 'In the beginning of God's preparing the heavens and the earth, the earth then has existed waste and void,' and has no reference to the original creation of matter, but to a subsequent formation, probably referred to also in Pr. 8.26, 'while He hath not the earth, or the outplaces, or the *highest part* of the dusts of the (habitable or fruit-bearing) world.' See also v. 23, of the same chapter: 'of old I have been set up (*or* anointed, see Ps. 2.6,) from the beginning, from former states of the earth.' Contrary to all Hebrew idiom is the translation of some, 'first of all, *or* in the first place, God,' &c. [Emphases his throughout, but the words in square brackets are my own.]"[22]

---

[22] Young, Robert, *Concise Critical Comments On The Holy Bible*,

It should be pointed out that in spite of Robert Young's comments above, it is most definitely the norm for grammarians, both Jewish and Christian, to regard *bara*, בָּרָא, as a verb rather than a noun. Of course were it to be regarded as a noun, then undoubtedly it would bolster the Construct State/Dependent Clause view, but, as we have seen, even Snaith, a champion of the Dependent Clause view regarded *bara*, בָּרָא, as a verb, and made the Absolute from an entire phrase, (*created God the heavens and the earth*). It should also be noted that with Genesis 1:1, we are dealing with the most fundamental statement of all, the very creation of the space-time-matter universe, an event that not only is truly without parallel, but which by its nature could never have any parallel. This means that Robert Young's doubts about this one instance being understood differently from the other occurrences of *reshith*, רֵאשִׁית, are unfounded; an *unique* event might well call for an unique literary form to describe it.

It has also been suggested that had Moses intended to refer to the Absolute Beginning of everything in Genesis 1:1, he would have used the word *t'ghilah*, תְּחִלָּה, *beginning*, which it is claimed is used absolutely, but this view is incorrect I believe. Roddy has demonstrated that *t'ghilah*, תְּחִלָּה, *beginning* "denotes a beginning relative to the time of speaking not an absolute beginning as some claim", and cites Genesis 13:3; 41:21; 43:18–20; and Isaiah 1:26 as evidence [Emphasis original].[23] A complete concordance of *t'ghilah*, תְּחִלָּה, *beginning*, is given in Appendix II and seems to confirm Roddy's view.

London, Pickering & Inglis, undated, in.loc.

[23] Roddy, A. J., in the article, *Exegesis Of Genesis 1:1,2.*, in *Scripture Research* Volume 2, Number 16, Atascadero, California, Ewalt Memorial Bible School Incorporated, undated. pp. 495ff.

Is בראשית an Absolute?

Keil and Delitzsch in their commentary on the Pentateuch robustly assert that *bereshith*, בראשית, is used Absolutely in Genesis 1:1, while admitting it might be used relatively on occasions. In their view *bereshith*, בראשית, is used as is the phrase, *In beginning*, εν αρχη, in John 1:1, and *mareshith*, מראשית, *from the beginning*, in Isaiah 46:10, that is, as an Absolute. They add that the next clause cannot be regarded as what they call *a subordinate*, which is another term for *Dependent*, either by translating it, *in the beginning when God created..., the earth was*, or as, *in the beginning when God created... (but the earth was then a chaos, etc.), God said, Let there be light*, as advocated by both Ewald and Bunsen. Making the very same point as Cassuto and E. J. Young recorded above, they point out that the first rendering is impossible owing to the rules of Hebrew grammar, which would demand that verse 2 should commence, *and without form the earth*, ותהי הארץ. They then add that the second rendering would be conspicuously at odds with what they term "the simplicity of style which pervades the whole chapter", remarking that this particular "construction is invented for the simple purpose of getting rid of the doctrine of a *creatio ex nihilo*, [creation-out-of-nothing] which is so repulsive to modern Pantheism." They conclude by saying that *reshith*, ראשית, is a relative concept, and refers to the propagation or initiation of a series of incidents or objects, but add that the setting in which it is found in Genesis 1:1 identifies it as denoting "the very first beginning, the commencement of the world, when time itself began." [The words in square brackets are my own.][24]

---

[24] Keil, C. F., and Delitzsch, F., *Commentary On The Old Testament*, Volume I, Grand Rapids, Michigan, U.S.A., Eerdmans, pp. 46–47.

Edward J. Young is in complete agreement with this sentiment. He observes that when in the Old Testament a finite verb is preceded by a Construct, it is signalled to the reader either by the context, or by the form of the word. Young gives as an example of the latter, Hosea 1:2, which reads, *The beginning of the speaking of the Lord,* תחלת רבד יהוה. The word translated. *The beginning,* תחלת reveals clearly through its *form* that it is a Construct.[25] As an example of the Construct being indicated to the reader by the *context*, Young cites Exodus 6:28, *And it was on the day spoke...,* ויהי ביום דבר. The form of the word *day, yom,* יום, does not define whether the noun is an Absolute or a Construct, but the context shows unequivocally that it must be understood as a Construct. However, Young points out that when we turn to Genesis 1:1, neither the form of the word or the context requires *bereshith,* בראשית, to be considered as a Construct, in fact, the opposite is true. Not only does the context not require the presence of a Construct; it seems indisputably to require an Absolute.[26]

It should also be pointed out that the Septuagint translates Genesis 1:1 as Εν αρχη εποιησεν ο θεος τον ουρανον και την γην, *In beginning made God the heaven and the earth...*[27] This is often taken by supporters of the Absolute-State/Independent Clause view, as supporting their case, especially as John's Gospel also opens with the words Εν αρχη, that is, *In beginning.* This is translated *bereshith,* בראשית, in both of the Hebrew New Testaments I have at my

---

[25] The final ת of תחלת indicates it is a Construct form of תחלה ,as does the pointing. See Davidson, op.cit., in.loc., and Kelley, *Biblical Hebrew: An Introductory Grammar,* op.cit., § 26.4 (2) (h), p. 62.

[26] Young, E. J., op.cit., p. 6.

[27] *The Septuagint With Apocrypha: Greek And English,* translated Brenton, Sir Lancelot C. L., Peabody, Massachusetts, U.S.A., Hendrickson, 1997, in.loc.

disposal.[28] Theologically it seems impossible to conceive of anything before the *Beginning* of John 1:1, apart from the Presence of the Persons of the Godhead. Thus the occurrence of *bereshith*, בראשית, here in Hebrew versions of John 1:1, which has interesting parallels with Genesis 1:1 of course, shows that it may indeed be used Absolutely.

Examples of ראשית in the Absolute State

Supporters of the Absolute State/Independent Clause view also point out that *reshith*, ראשית, is undoubtedly in the Absolute State in Leviticus 2:12, where it is also anarthrous, and lacks a preposition; and in Nehemiah 12:44, where it does have a preposition, this time ל (*over*) rather than ב (*in*). Finally in Isaiah 46:10 it is again found without the article, in the Absolute State, and with an inseparable preposition, מ (*from*).[29]

Further slight evidence is to be derived from the accent used with בראשית in Genesis 1:1. Every word of the Hebrew text carries at least one accent, unless it is a word joined to another. What is known as the Primary Accent identifies the tone syllable of the word, which, usually is the final syllable. The accents however are also used as punctuation, and here two general categories need to be noted, namely; *conjunctive* and *disjunctive* accents. As their names indicate, the former *connect*, and the latter *separate*, and are used to indicate the syntactical relationships of individual words. The Masoretes have marked בראשית in Genesis 1:1 with what is known as a

---

[28] Although the pointing is slightly different. See *The New Testament In Hebrew And English*, Edgware, Middlesex, The Society For Distributing The Holy Scriptures To The Jews, undated, in.loc., and also ספרי הברית החדשה, London, The United Bible Societies, 1979, in.loc.

[29] Fields, op.cit., pp. 153ff.

Disjunctive Tiphcha (or *Tippha*, which is the mark ˎ seen underneath the שׁ of בראשׁית in the Masoretic text of Genesis 1:1). This is what is called a *subordinate disjunctive*. The two *primary disjunctives* are *Athnah*, which marks the end of the first half of a verse, and the *Silluq* which marks the end of the last half of the verse. The *Disjunctive Tiphcha* is in a category between these two, and gives the word בראשׁית its own independent accent, suggesting that the Masoretes regarded it as being in the Absolute State. Both Weston Fields and Edward J. Young make this point very clearly; although they rightly warn that the Masoretes were not infallible.[30]

Summary

So far then we have two possibilities;

1) Genesis 1:1 may be a Dependent Clause, with the main statement in verse 2 or 3. This would mean that the Creation described in Genesis 1 began with a pre-existing formless and waste earth, but we know nothing at all about the history of the time that preceded this creative work.

2) Genesis 1:1 is an Independent Clause, there is no history before the creation this verse refers to, as nothing outside the Godhead existed before the event it describes.

So far then there appear to be no grammatical reasons for rejecting either view, but the fact that *reshith*, ראשׁית, is in Scripture normally found in the Construct State, might be said to encourage the first view, giving the sense that there is an unrecorded history or chronological gap prior to Genesis 1:1.

---

[30] Ibid, p. 156, and Young, E. J., op.cit., p. 5. See Kelly, op.cit., pp. 16–18, and Gesenius, op.cit., § 15 *f* 5 for details.

Part B: ברא

We now turn to the second word of Genesis 1:1; *bara*, ברא. How should this be understood? There are three main views on this matter.

1) It is frequently stated by supporters of the Dependent Clause view that *bara*, ברא, means "to cut", and therefore implies that the creation of Genesis 1, was a working or fashioning of *pre-existing material*, namely the unformed and unfilled earth, which then was *cut* or *shaped* during the hexameron,[31] into the earth we now inhabit. According to this point-of-view *bara*, ברא, does not apply to the original creation of the earth (and heavens). It is frequently pointed out by such people that Joshua 17:15 proves this to be the case. This text reads, "Get thee up to the wood country, *and cut down* (ובראת) for thyself there."

2) On the other hand, those who place the Gap between Genesis 1:1 and 2 take the opposite view, saying that *bara*, ברא, refers to *creatio ex nihilo*,[32] while *asah*, עשה, used elsewhere in Genesis 1, means to *make from pre-existing material*, or to *appoint*, or to *make visible*. Such people point out that Exodus 20:11 speaks of the heaven and earth being *restored* during the six days of Genesis 1, as *asah*, עשה, is used in

---

[31] A hexameron is something made from six parts, and is the usual way for theologians to designate the six days of creation found in Genesis 1.

[32] Creation-out-of-nothing.

that verse, not *bara*, ברא.[33] (This view will be tested in Chapter Three).

3) Those who believe there is no gap anywhere, usually try to show that *bara*, ברא, and *asah*, עשה, may be used interchangeably. (This view will also be tested in Chapter Three).

We must now seek to untangle this mess, and, in so doing, I believe, we will resolve the questions concerning *bereshith*, בראשית, referred to above.

The meaning of ברא

As views 2) and 3) will be examined later, we turn now to view 1) above. It does indeed seem as if the root meaning of *bara*, ברא, is to *cut*; Gesenius,[34] Davidson,[35] and Davies,[36] all agree on this. But while this might seem to strengthen the hand of those who consider verse 1 to be a Dependent Clause, with *bereshith*, בראשית, a Construct, a word of caution is required. It is true to say that *bara*, ברא, does not mean *creatio-ex-nihilo*, but then, no word in Hebrew has this meaning, nor has any in English, or in any other language come to that. While I do not embrace all of Robert Young's views, I wholeheartedly agree with him when he wrote:

---

[33] In Appendix IV, I show every occurrence of ברא and עשה in Genesis 1.

[34] Gesenius, H. W. F., *Hebrew And Chaldee Lexicon Of The Old Testament Scriptures*, translated, Tregelles, S. P., Grand Rapids, Michigan, U.S.A., Baker Book House, 1984, based on Bagster's edition of 1847, in.loc.

[35] Op.cit., in.loc.

[36] Davies, Benjamin, *A Compendious And Complete Hebrew And Chaldee Lexicon To The Old Testament*, London, Asher and Co., 1889, in.loc.

> "To create from nothing is a phrase, and no language on earth, it is believed, can express it, save by a phrase."[37]

Thus, the fact that *bara*, ברא, means to *cut*, does not, by itself prove Genesis 1:1 is a Dependent Clause.

Further, Snaith,[38] Bagster's *Hebrew Student's Manual*,[39] Roddy,[40] and Fields,[41] all confirm that bara, ברא, in Genesis 1:1 is in the Qal (or Kal) form,[42] and, it has been noticed of *bara*, ברא, by several grammarians that it is only to be understood as to *cut* or *carve*, when it is in the Piel form.[43] Whenever it is in Qal, however, it means no such thing; instead, it means *to make* or *create*, but in a more restricted sense than either of these English words.

Edward J. Young in his book, *Studies In Genesis One*, emphasised the significant fact that whenever *bara*, ברא, is found in Qal, as it is in Genesis 1:1, it is applied exclusively to Divine activity. Furthermore, the concepts of novelty, or of an unexpected, or highly unusual consequence of this Divine

---

[37] Op.cit., p. 1.

[38] Op.cit., in.loc.

[39] Op.cit., p. 1 of the *Hebrew Reading Lessons*.

[40] Op.cit., p. 499.

[41] Op.cit., p. 54.

[42] Qal is the *simple* or *light* form of the verb, not being weighted with additional qualifying consonants.

[43] Davidson, op.cit., in.loc, Gesenius, *Hebrew-Chaldee Lexicon To The Old Testament*, op.cit., in.loc, Keil and Delitzsch, op.cit., p. 47, Fields, op.cit., p. 54, Roddy, op.cit., p. 499, and Strong, A. H., *Systematic Theology: A Compendium Designed For The Use Of Theological Students*, London, Pickering & Inglis, 1981, p. 376. Gesenius, *Hebrew Grammar*, op.cit., p. 141, defines the meaning of the Piel conjugation, is that of busying oneself eagerly with the idea conveyed by the stem, thus acting as an intensive.

activity are frequently associated with its use. Another significant feature of the use of *bara*, ברא, in Qal is that while it is found with the accusative of the product, no raw material is ever mentioned. Young gives as an example the fact that while we are told that in Genesis 1:27 God created (*bara*, ברא) man, we are not told that God created man *from the dust of the ground*.[44] Young argues from this interesting fact, that the word *bara*, ברא, has a more restricted use than the English word *create*. He also observes, that these points demonstrate that if in Genesis 1:1 it was Moses' intention to convey to the reader the concept of Absolute Creation, no other word in the Hebrew language would have been more suitable to his purpose. With this I agree wholeheartedly. Thus, when *bara*, ברא, is found together with *bereshith*, בראשית, according to Young we should understand it to mean,

> "The beginning was by means of a creative act."[45]

W. Fields cites Gesenius on this matter who notes how the use of *bara*, ברא, in Qal is completely different from what he terms "its primitive signification (to cut, to shape, to fashion)", being used instead to indicate the creation of something *utterly novel*, rather than the processing of raw material. Gesenius adds that Genesis 1:1 therefore asserts that the earth was originally created from nothing in a state totally lacking in order, and that the rest of the chapter describes the steps which brought it into a state of orderliness by the working and moving of the substances of which the world consisted.[46]

---

[44] Instead we are told in Genesis 2:7 that the Lord God *formed*, (*yahtsar* יצר) Adam from the dust of the ground.

[45] Op.cit., pp. 6–7.

[46] Gesenius, *Thesaurus Linguae Hebr. Et Chald*, Leipzig, Vogel, 1829, I., p. 236a, cited in Fields, op.cit., pp. 54–55.

Keil and Delitzsch in their commentary on the Pentateuch concur, pointing out that *bara*, ברא, in Piel in Joshua 17:15–18, means *to cut*, or *to hew*, but in Qal, as it is in Genesis 1:1, it is without exception used of creation by God; "the production of that which had no existence before", adding, that it is then never found with an accusative of any material. They add that within Genesis 1 it:

> "is used for the creation of man (ver. 27. ch. v. 1, 2), and of everything new that God creates, whether in the Kingdom of nature (Num. xvi. 30) or of that of grace (Ex. xxxiv. 10; Ps. lI. 10, etc.). In this verse, however, the existence of any primeval material is precluded by the object created: "the heavens and the earth.""[47]

Augustus Hopkins Strong is of like mind. Citing Guyot he points out that in Genesis 1,

> "[*Bara*] ברא is used (1) of the creation of the universe (1:1); (2) of the creation of the great sea monsters (1:21); (3) of the creation of man (1:27). Everywhere else we read of God's *making*, as from an already created substance, the firmament (1:7), the sun. moon and stars (1:16), the brute creation (1:25); or of his *forming* the beasts of the field out of the ground (2:19); or, lastly, of his *building up* into a woman the rib he had taken from man (2:22 margin)."[48]

Thus, *bara*, ברא, is reserved for the initial creation of Spiritual Life, represented by man, the initial creation of sentient beings, represented by the sea monsters, indicating

---

[47] Op.cit., p. 47.
[48] Guyot, cited in Strong, op.cit., p. 374.

34

that its use in Genesis 1:1, is in connection with the initial creation of the third great division of the creation; the space-time-matter universe.[49] Strong adds that *bara*, בְּרָא,

> "signifies the production of an effect for which no natural antecedent existed before, and which can only be the result of divine agency. For this reason, in the Kal species it is used only of God, and is never accompanied by any accusative denoting material."[50]

Finally, Sarna, like the previous commentators notes the fact that whenever it is found in Qal, *bara*, בְּרָא, signifies the Divine creation of something entirely new and unprecedented; which cannot be emulated by human activity; and which displays no reference to raw material. He then goes on to examine the doctrine of *creation ex nihilo*, and writes:

> "As Ibn Ezra observed, *bara'* does not of itself denote the creation of something out of nothing (*creation ex nihilo*). This doctrine seems to have been first articulated in the late Second Temple work, 2 Maccabees: "Look up to heaven and earth and see all that is therein, and know that God made them out of things that did not exist" (7:28). However, the Genesis narrative does contain intimations of such a concept. Precisely because of the indispensable importance of pre-existing matter in the pagan cosmologies, the very absence of such mention here is highly

---

[49] This is not to say that the angelic hosts were not already in existence before man was created, but merely to point out that man is the first example of spiritual life that is referred to. With the creation of the heavens and earth for which no pre-existing material seems to be available, there could be no similar situation however.

[50] Strong, op.cit., pp. 374–375.

significant. This conclusion is reinforced by the idea of creation by divine fiat without reference to any inert matter being present. Also, the repeated biblical emphasis upon God as the exclusive Creator would seem to rule out the possibility of pre-existent matter. Finally, if *bara'* is used only of God's creation, it must be essentially distinct from human creation. The ultimate distinction would be *creatio ex nihilo*, which has no human parallel and is thus utterly beyond all human comprehension."[51]

בראשית *and* ברא

Now the Hebrew Traditionalists have often pointed out that the first word of Scripture, *bereshith*, בְּרֵאשִׁית, actually *contains* the second word, *bara*, ברא. This is taken as indicating how closely associated the Beginning, and Creation are; how the moment of Beginning *contains* the Creation; or how Creation *emerges* from the Beginning. Amongst gentile commentators, Edward J. Young is the only person I have come across who has noticed this fact, and seen its significance. He states,

> "We may approach a consideration of this context by noting the alliteration with which the Bible begins. The sequence א ר ב א of בְּרֵאשִׁית appears again in the verb ברא. This would seem to tie up the concept expressed by בראשית with that of ברא... The beginning and unique creation—namely, that of heaven and earth—are here joined together. Hence, we may understand the writer as asserting that the

---

[51] Op.cit., p. 5.

heaven and earth had a beginning and that this beginning is to be found in the fact that God had created them."[52]

The Transcendent God

The impact of these considerations is enormous, seemingly shutting out the possibility of Genesis 1:1 being a Dependent Clause, by eliminating the possibility of raw-material that is utterly essential for the viability of the Dependent Clause view. But it is also of immense theological impact, allowing us to see that Genesis 1:1 reveals to us a Creator Whom later passages of Scripture reveal to be Imminent within His Creation (Jeremiah 23:24, "Do not I fill heaven and earth saith the Lord"), *is also Transcendentally Above and Beyond it.* Just as God was not acting with pre-existent matter at the Beginning of Genesis 1:1, neither was He acting within space or time when He initiated the Beginning, for at that moment of initiation, space, matter, and time were not. Therefore His action of initiating the Beginning occurred outside of space and time, and independently of matter, which were themselves only created at the Beginning, elevating God in our minds, enabling us to conceive of His Transcendence to all that we know. In initiating the Beginning He acted independently of space, time, and matter.

Augustine of Hippo writing in the fifth century C.E. was acutely aware of this. He said,

> "The Bible says (and the Bible never lies); 'In the beginning God made heaven and earth.' It must be inferred that God had created nothing before that; 'in the beginning' must refer to whatever He made before all His other works.

---

[52] Op.cit., pp. 6–7.

> Thus there can be no doubt that the world was not created in time but with time. An event in time happens after one time and before another, after the past and before the future. But at the time of creation there could have been no past, because there was nothing created to provide the change and movement which is the condition of time."[53]

Nahum Sarna, commented on the usual English rendering of Genesis 1:1, *In the beginning God created the heaven and the earth*, which views the phrase as an Independent Statement of Absolute Creation, He shows how this translation understands the first word, *bereshith*, בראשית, as signifying,

> "at the beginning of time"

and observed that this marked

> "a momentous assertion about the nature of God: that He is wholly outside of time, just as He is outside of space, both of which He proceeds to create. In other words, for the first time in the religious history of the Near East, God is conceived as being entirely free of temporal and spatial dimensions."[54]

It is important to note here, the elevating and ennobling effect upon our theology, granted by sound exegesis.

'Creation-Ex-Nihilo', or 'Ex-Creation'?

Nahum Sarna refers to II Maccabees 7:28 as delineating the doctrine of *creatio ex nihilo*, but he could also have referred to

---

[53] Augustine of Hippo, *The City Of God*, translated Bettenson, Harmondsworth, Penguin Books, 1977, Book XI, Chapter 6.

[54] Op.cit., p. 5.

some Christian Scriptures, (had it not been the case that he is a Jewish exegete writing for fellow Jewish believers), which seem to give a still more sophisticated viewpoint. Hebrews 11:3 reads,

> "Through faith, we understand that the worlds were framed by the Word of God, so that things which are seen were not made of things which do appear."

There are those who might suggest in spite of its contradicting the context of this verse, that this could still be understood as a reference to raw material as the things which do not appear could be sub-atomic particles. The next text however shows clearly how Hebrews 11:3 should be understood. In Romans 11:36 we find the following,

> "For of Him, and through Him, and to Him, are all things."

The words "of Him" are actually in the Greek text, "εξ αυτου," "*out of Whom...*" (are) All Things! That means the space-time-matter universe and all it contains came *out* from God. *The Concordant Version* correctly translates this verse

> "Seeing that all is out of Him."[55]

This compares well with John Bowes' rendition,

> "Out of Him... are all things."[56]

---

[55] The *Consistent Emphasised Version*, found in the *Concordant Version: The Sacred Scriptures*, translated Knoch, Los Angeles, The Concordant Publishing Concern, revised edition 1930, in.loc. This is almost identical to the *Uniform Sublinear* found in the same work. *The Sacred Scriptures: Concordant Literal New Testament*, (Canyon County, California, U.S.A., The Concordant Publishing Concern, sixth edition of 1976), is also almost identical.

As my first instructor in the Scriptures, the linguist A. G. Tilney long ago said, we see here _ex-creation_, for the words εξ αυτου... τα παντα, mean literally "out of Whom... the universe."[57] Thus, contrary to what is commonly thought, the words of Scripture do not teach _creatio-ex-nihilo_, for God is not nothing! God is _Infinite_, therefore, the universe, or "the heavens and the earth" to use the designation of Genesis 1:1 came _out_ from the Infinite resources of the Godhead, explaining the absence of raw material for which there was never any need.

Summary

It seems then that there are no grammatical obstacles to viewing Genesis 1:1 as an Independent Statement. The article which is absent from _bereshith_, בראשׁית, is unnecessary, as it is an adverbial reference to a temporal event. It is indeed true that _reshith_, ראשׁית, is almost always used as a Construct, and that on every other occasion of _reshith_, ראשׁית, where it is joined with the inseparable preposition _in_, ב, to form _bereshith_, בראשׁית, it is indubitably a Construct, but the Creation of the Heavens and the Earth is of course an absolutely unique event, indeed, an unique _kind_ of event, and we might expect to find an unique, but perfectly legitimate grammatical form used in relating it therefore. Edward J. Young has pointed out, as was seen earlier, that the Masoretes have accented _bereshith_, בראשׁית, in Genesis 1:1 with the _Disjunctive Tiphcha_, suggesting it is truly an Absolute, making Genesis 1:1 an Independent Statement. Robert Young, who believes the text to be a Dependent Clause points out that there is only one passage in the entire Hebrew

---

[56] _The New Testament Translated From The Purest Greek_, translated Bowes, Dundee, published privately by the author, 1870, in.loc.

[57] Tilney, A. G., _Redefinitions Of Biblical Terms And Phrases_, published privately by the author, undated, p. 5.

Canon where *reshith*, ראשׁית, is used Absolutely, in reference to a temporal event, lacks the article, and is joined to an inseparable preposition. This one other occasion is to be found in Isaiah 46:10, but when we look at this verse, we find that it too is an unmistakable reference to *The Beginning* of Genesis 1:1. Thus Robert Young actually shows the extreme likelihood of Genesis 1:1 being an Independent Clause! Further, the fact that *bara*, ברא, in this verse is in the Qal form increases still more the likelihood of Genesis 1:1 being an Independent Statement, especially as it is connected to *bereshith*, בראשׁית, by the alliteration found in the first two words of the text as Edward J. Young and the Hebrew Traditionalists point out.

Conclusion 1. Genesis 1:1 is an Independent Clause relating the Absolute Beginning of the universe that was brought forth by the Creator from the infinite resources of the Godhead.

Conclusion 2. It is impossible to conceive of any period of time before the initiation of the Beginning of Genesis 1:1, therefore there can be no gap prior to Genesis 1:1.

Conclusion to Chapter 1

Understanding Genesis 1:1 correctly has two major consequences. Firstly, as we saw it allows us to conceive of the Transcendence of God, a fact which helps us in our contemplation of the "Above" of Ephesians 1:21, 2:6, and Colossians 3:1. Secondly it eliminates any possibility of a gap prior to Genesis 1:1, but it does this through *seemingly* loosening the ties between verse 1, and verses 2 and 3 that those who embrace the Dependent Clause view would seek to establish. Thus, inevitably, having only just begun our investigation, Genesis 1:1 *appears* to be separate from verse 2, and all that follows on. There are those who, understanding that verse 1 and verses 2–3 are not joined by clause dependency, attempt to lever apart verses 1 and 2, in order to create room for the insertion of a gap between them, which, like the alleged gap before verse 1, might then be used to accommodate evolutionary epochs, the Luciferic Fall, or, both. It is to this subject that we now turn.

Chapter Two

Is there a gap between Genesis 1:1 and 1:2?

With verse 2 of Genesis 1 we approach the very centre of the controversy. The earth is described as being waste and void. Was this the earth's original condition? or, was it a state it had entered after being ruined during or following the Luciferic Fall? To examine this matter, this chapter is divided into three parts. In Part A I examine the initial word *wahaerets*, והארץ; in Part B, the second word *hayetha*, היתה; and in Part 3, the phrase *thohu wabhohu* תהו ובהו. I summarise the results of this at the conclusion of this chapter.

Part A והארץ

As with Genesis 1:1, we begin this Chapter by considering the very first word of the verse in question. This word is *wahaerets*, והארץ, and it is a matter of supreme importance to understand how this word must be understood. The problem actually centres upon the very first letter of this word, the Hebrew conjunction *waw*, ו. Nobody challenges how the rest of the word *haerets*,, הארץ, should be translated of course. Unquestionably, it means *the earth*, but the conjunction *waw*, ו, may be translated in many ways, including *and*, *but*, *now*, or *then*.[58] If it is to be understood here as meaning *but*, as many Gap Theorists affirm, then we have the first piece of real

---

[58] Gesenius, H. W. F., *Hebrew And Chaldee Lexicon*, op.cit., in.loc.

43

evidence that there might be a gap between Genesis 1:1 and 1:2, as it would allow the thought that something had happened to *change* the earth after its creation in verse 1, and prior to the hexameron, which commences in verse 3.

Genesis 1:2a as a Noun-Clause

A very real clue indicating how we are to understand *waw* ו at this point is provided by the context of this word *wahaerets*, והארץ. It must form a part of either a noun-clause or a verbal-clause. Under the heading of "The Sentence," H. W. F. Gesenius defines these clauses thus;

> "1. Every sentence, the subject and predicate of which are nouns or their equivalents (esp. particles), is called a *noun-clause*, e.g. יהוה מלכנו *the Lord is our king*, Is 33[22]; ואנשי סדם רעים וחטאים *now the men of Sodom were wicked and sinners*, Gn 13[13]; פה להם *a mouth is theirs*, Ψ 115[5]... 2. Every sentence, the subject of which is a noun (or pronoun included in a verbal form) and its predicate a finite verb, is called a *verbal-clause*, e.g. ויאמר אלהים *and God said*, Gn 1[3]; ויבדל *and he divided*, 1[7]."[59]

It would seem that the crucial importance of this distinction cannot be over-emphasised. Shortly after defining the sentence types referred to above, Gesenius goes on to emphasise with particular force how vitally important it is to understand the difference between them, and especially the difference between the clause types. Gesenius insists it is absolutely essential to grasp these facts in order to understand with clarity and precision the exact meaning of the Hebrew text. He states that these distinctions are not just external, but reveal,

---

[59] Gesenius, *Hebrew Grammar*, op.cit., p. 450.

"*fundamental differences of meaning*. Noun-clauses with a substantive as predicate, represent something *fixed, a state* or in short, *a being* so and so; verbal-clauses on the other hand, something *movable* and *in progress*, an *event* or *action* (emphasis mine)."[60]

Thorleif Boman, who has produced a major work on Hebrew thought, also entirely endorses this view of the rôle of the noun-clause.[61]

Now it could not be easier to decide which type of clause we are dealing with in Genesis 1:2a. The subject is *haerets*, הארץ, *the earth*; the predicate is *thohu wabhohu*, תהו ובהו, *without form and void*. Thus, clearly we a dealing with a noun-clause here, as, incidentally, Gesenius happens to note himself citing Genesis 1:2a as an *example* of a noun-clause.[62] It might be thought that the presence of *hayetha*, היתה, *was*, here might change things, meaning that Genesis 1:2a ought to be considered as a verbal clause after all. There are occasions where *hayah*, היה, is used as a fully-fledged verb, while on other occasions it is used only as a copula to join subject and predicate, or to refer to a past or future time, but again Gesenius actually refutes this directly by saying that Genesis 1:2a is not one of these special cases. Gesenius insists that *hayetha*, היתה, is employed in this verse simply because it is a reference to the past. There will be more on this point in Part B of this Chapter.[63]

Conclusion 3. Genesis 1:2a is a noun-clause.

---

[60] Ibid.

[61] Boman, Thorleif, *Hebrew Thought Compared With Greek*, London, SCM Press, p. 35.

[62] Gesenius, *Hebrew Grammar*, op.cit., p. 452, footnote 2.

[63] Ibid., p. 454.

Now, it is an interesting fact, that with noun-clauses, the first noun occupies the place of emphasis. The first noun in Genesis 1:2a is of course, *haerets*, הָאָרֶץ, *the earth*, giving a special emphasis to our earth. Fields, after pointing out the significance of this rule of Hebrew grammar for the accurate exegesis of Genesis 1:1–2, explains that the emphasis given to the first noun of a noun clause is the equivalent of using italicised print in an English language publication, or underlining in a typewritten work. He adds:

> "Genesis 1:2, thus, might be paraphrased in this manner; "Now as far as the earth was concerned, it was…""[64]

Joseph Bryant Rotherham produced his own translation of the Scriptures, which he entitled *The Emphasised Version*, because he incorporated into his translation the special forms of emphasis embedded within the Hebrew and Greek texts which the ordinary English reader would not notice. This is of peculiar benefit to students of the Scriptures, and it is of interest to note that Rotherham here, because of the grammatical rules just discussed, translated Genesis 1:2a as Fields suggests, "Now the earth…" In a footnote Rotherham remarks, "The emphasis on "the earth" in ver. 2 is quite regular… The effect of it here is to single out "the earth" from ver. 1 for special comment."[65]

In common with many other commentators, Edward J. Young draws the attention of his readers to the emphasis given to the word *haerets*, הָאָרֶץ, because it is the initial noun within a noun clause, and explains that this emphasis means that from that point on, we must focus our attention upon the earth,

---

[64] Op.cit., p. 78.

[65] *The Emphasised Bible: A New Translation*, translated by Rotherham, J. B., Cincinnati, The Standard Publishing Company, 1916, in.loc.

which now becomes 'centre-stage' for the rest of the chapter, and of the rest of Scripture. The earth on which we live and die, becomes the focus for the Scriptures which illuminate the lives lived upon it. Young then in a footnote cites Keil who says,

> "Though treating of the creation of the heaven and the earth, the writer, both here and in what follows, describes with minuteness the original condition and progressive formation of the earth alone, and says nothing more respecting the heaven than is actually requisite in order to show its connection with the earth. He is writing for inhabitants of the earth, and for religious ends; not to gratify curiosity, but to strengthen faith in God, the creator of the universe."[66]

In Chapter One, the alliteration of *bereshith bara*, בראשית ברא, was noted, together with the fact that it draws the two words together. Now the syntactical relationship of Genesis 1:1 and 1:2 is, for me, just as intriguing, as the word *haerets*, הארץ, occurs twice in succession, separated only by the conjunction *waw*, ו, as *haerets*, הארץ, is the last word of verse 1, and the first word of verse 2, as the interlinear in the Introduction shows. We noted in Chapter One, above, that viewing verse 1 as an Independent Clause had the effect of drawing it away from verses 2 and 3, allowing Gap Theorists to attempt to lever open a space between verses 1 and 2, in which their gap might then be located. But the twofold occurrence of *haerets*, הארץ, at this very point, has the opposite effect, drawing together these two verses in the most intimate manner, the 'join' then being eliminated by the *nail*, or *hook* of the conjunction ו, waw (the meaning of the letter[67]).

---

[66] Op.cit., pp. 31–32.

[67] Steele-Smith, *Wonders Of The Hebrew Alphabet*, Sydney, The Central Press, undated, p. 33.

We see here, as with the alliteration of *bereshith bara*, בראשית ברא, what Jewish exegetes call an exegetical *hint*[68] at a truth not stated directly in the text, but true nonetheless Our next piece of evidence shows this view to be justified I believe.

Genesis 1:2a as a Circumstantial Clause

Returning to the context of *wahaerets*, והארץ, we have seen in the most clear manner imaginable that it is part of a noun-clause, the function of which relates to the description of a *static* or *fixed* condition, and that it cannot possibly refer to a condition brought about by *change* of any kind. But, in addition to this, the clause of Genesis 1:2a, is also what is known as a circumstantial clause. To quote from Gesenius again, he informs us that:

> "The statement of the particular circumstances under which a subject appears as performing some action, or under which an action (or an occurrence) is accomplished, is made especially (apart from relative clauses...) by means of noun-clauses connected by *Waw* with a following subject."[69]

This is precisely what we find with *wahaerets*, והארץ! It is, as we have seen unequivocally, a part of a noun-clause, connected by *waw*, ו, and with a subject, *haerets*, הארץ, following. This fact, and the implications for the demise of the Gap Theory, were noted long ago by F. F. Bruce,[70] and represent the most serious challenge for the Gap Theory that

---

[68] Stern D., *The Jewish New Testament Commentary*, Clarksville, Maryland, U.S.A., Jewish New Testament Publications, sixth edition 1999, pp. 11ff.

[69] Op.cit., p. 489.

[70] See Fields, op.cit., p. 79.

we have seen so far. It is this consideration that has driven many Gap Theorists, including no less a scholar than Merrill Unger, to place the alleged gap before Genesis 1:1, which, we have already ruled out by our previous findings. Such people understand with clarity that the existence of a circumstantial noun-clause in Genesis 1:2a virtually eliminates the possibility of any gap between Genesis 1:1 and 1:2.[71]

Fields sums up the consequences for the exegesis of Genesis 1:2, that flow from the realisation that it is a circumstantial noun-clause, as realised by competent grammarians, as follows:

> "By circumstantial sentences we mean such as, following a noun or pronoun (the latter may also be included in the verb) describe the *condition* or circumstances in which the person or thing denoted by the noun or pronoun was at the time of the principle action."

We conclude, therefore, that Genesis 1:2a consists of a noun clause which is circumstantial (subordinate and explanatory) to the main verb of 1:1. This means that 1:2a is *a description of the earth as it was created originally*, not how it became at a time subsequent to creation. This much can be concluded on the basis of the meaning of the circumstantial noun clause alone.[72]

Conclusion 4. Genesis 1:2a is a circumstantial noun-clause.

---

[71] Ibid.

[72] Ibid., p. 80. The citation made by Fields is from Muller, A., *Outlines Of Hebrew Syntax*, Glasgow, James Maclehose & Sons, 1888, p. 101.

Waw ו

We now need to consider what form the conjunction *waw*, ו, assumes in this particular case. Gap Theorists believe it to be a waw-consecutive, which implies a sequence of events is under consideration. Event 2, follows on from Event 1, and is introduced by the waw-consecutive. This would mean, of course, that verse 2 would be seen, using the simple example above, as Event 2, and would be placed chronologically *after* Event 1, which would be the Absolute Creation of verse 1. This, of course would allow the existence of a gap, but would contradict our previous findings which have identified verse 2a as a circumstantial noun-clause. The question to ask then is, is it at all possible that the waw in, *wahaerets*, והארץ is consecutive?

This is what Gesenius says of the waw-consecutive:

> "This name best expresses the prevailing syntactical relation, for by *waw-consecutive* an action is always represented as the direct, or at least temporal *consequence* of a preceding action. Moreover... the waw-consecutive can only be thus used in immediate conjunction with the verb."[73]

It is unquestionably the case that the waw under consideration is connected not with a verb, but with a noun, *haerets*, הארץ, *the earth*, and therefore may not be *consecutive* at all, but must be instead, *waw-copulative*, which is never attached to a verb, and is used to add further information about the subject. This is what we would expect given that verse 2a has already been identified as a circumstantial noun-clause. The waw thus forms a special type of copulative, called by Gesenius, the

---

[73] *Hebrew Grammar*, op.cit., p. 133, footnote 1. See also *The Hebrew Student's Manual*, op.cit., p. 54.

explicative, which *explains* some quality or characteristic of the subject previously mentioned, by adding further details.[74]

F. F. Bruce who was keenly aware of this problem for the Gap Theory stated that if the Gap Theory were true, then we would indeed expect to find the waw-consecutive at the beginning of verse 2, rather that the waw-copulative that is present.[75] Weston Fields challenges Gap Theorists by asserting that if, as all the standard Hebrew grammars and lexicons confirm, Genesis 1:2 is truly an explanatory circumstantial noun clause, and therefore must be taken as describing conditions produced as a consequence of the action of the main verb (in verse 1), then it is unequivocally the end of the road for the Gap Theory. This is because, as Fields emphasises firmly, the Gap Theory must insist that Genesis 1:2 refers to conditions found subsequent to the action of the main verb, even though this is grammatically an impossibility. The grammatical facts of Genesis 1:2 drive us to conclude that the earth was *created* in a condition the Scriptures describe as *unformed and unfilled*. The Gap Theory contradicts these plain facts, and consequently, contradicts Scripture![76]

Conclusion 5. The waw of *wahaerets*, וְהָאָרֶץ, in Genesis 1:2a is copulative, not consecutive. This means it is in grammatical harmony with the findings stated in Conclusions 3, and 4, above, and introduces a statement that will explain further details about the creation of the earth referred to in verse 1.

---

[74] *Hebrew Grammar*, op.cit., p. 484.

[75] See Fields, op.cit., p. 85.

[76] Ibid., pp. 85–86.

היתה Part B

Gap Theorists routinely maintain that *hayetha*, היתה, in Genesis 1:2, should be translated as *became*, because their beliefs dictate that the condition of *thohu wabhohu*, תהו ובהו, *without form and void*, is not how the earth was created, but is a consequence of the Luciferic Fall. However, absolutely everything we have discovered so far about *wahaerets*, והארץ, indicates, unequivocally, that *hayetha*, היתה, the Qal perfect third person feminine singular of *hayah*, היה, *to be*,[77] should be translated as *was*.

We have just seen that:

1) because Genesis 1:2a is a <u>noun-clause</u>, the condition of *thohu wabhohu*, תהו ובהו, *without form and void*, must be a *static* condition, rather than a condition of the earth that was caused by some kind of *change*;

2) because Genesis 1:2a is a <u>circumstantial noun-clause</u>, it describes the consequence of the activity associated with the verb of the previous verse;

3) because Genesis 1:2a is an <u>explanatory circumstantial noun-clause</u>, it provides further information about the activity associated with the verb of the previous verse.

It would be extremely incongruous then with all that we have uncovered so far, if *hayetha*, היתה, were to be translated as anything but *was*.

Now it is both interesting and significant to note that speaking generally, translators, who are acutely aware of these facts, are opposed to Gap Theorists on this point, as the overwhelming

---

[77] Snaith, op.cit., in.loc.

majority of versions I have consulted render *hayetha*, הָיְתָה, at this point as *was*. I give the results of a brief survey of translations in the table below.

Version	Translation
A Literal Translation Of The Bible, by Jay P. Green Sr.[78]	being
A New Translation Of The Bible, by James Moffatt.[79]	was
Bagster's Hebrew Students Manual (Interlinear English Version in a test passage.)[80]	was
Brenton's English Version of *The Septuagint*.[81]	was
Frey's *A Hebrew Grammar In The English Language* (English translation in a test passage.)[82]	was
The American Standard Version.[83]	was
The Authorised King James Version[84].	was
The Bible In Basic English.[85]	was

---

[78] Being a part of *The Interlinear Bible: Hebrew-Greek-English*, Peabody, Massachusetts, U.S.A., Hendrickson, 1985.

[79] *A New Translation Of The Bible*, translated, James Moffatt, London, Hodder & Stoughton, Revised Edition, 1934.

[80] Op.cit., Part II, *A Series Of Hebrew Reading Lessons*, by S. P. Tregelles, pp. 1–2.

[81] *The Septuagint With Apocrypha: Greek And English*, translated Brenton, Peabody, Massachusetts, U.S.A., Hendrickson, 1997, based on the 1851 edition by Bagster.

[82] Frey, *A Hebrew Grammar In The English Language*, London, Henry G. Bohn, 1859, p. 125.

[83] *The Holy Bible*, Nashville, Thomas Nelson, 1929.

[84] *The Authorised King James Version*, Oxford, The University Press, undated.

[85] *The Bible In Basic English*, Cambridge, The University Press, 1965.

Version	Translation
The Concordant Version. [86]	became
The Emphasised Version, by J. B. Rotherham. [87]	became
The Good News Bible (Today's English Version) [88]	was
The Holy Bible: A Translation From The Latin Vulgate In The Light Of The Hebrew And Greek Originals, by Knox. (Roman Catholic, used only for reference). [89]	was
The Holy Bible In Modern English, translated by Ferrari Fenton. [90]	was
The Holy Bible Translated From The Latin Vulgate And Diligently Compared With The Hebrew, Greek, And Other Editions In Divers Languages, (Roman Catholic, used only for reference). [91]	was
The Holy Bible With Twenty Thousand Emendations. [92]	was

---

[86] *The Concordant Version Of The Old Testament*, Canyon Country, California, U.S.A., The Concordant Publishing Concern, 1957.

[87] Op.cit.

[88] *The Good News Bible: Today's English Version*, London, Collins/Fontana, 1976.

[89] *The Holy Bible: A Translation From The Latin Vulgate In The Light Of The Hebrew And Greek Originals*, translated Knox, London, Burns & Oates, 1963.

[90] *The Holy Bible In Modern English*, translated Ferrar Fenton, London, A. & C. Black, 1938.

[91] *The Holy Bible Translated From The Latin Vulgate And Diligently Compared With The Hebrew, Greek, And Other Editions In Divers Languages*, London, Burns & Oates, undated.

[92] *The Holy Bible With Twenty Thousand Emendations*, London, Longman, Brown & Co., 1843.

Version	Translation
The 'Holy Scriptures:' A New Translation From The Original Languages, by J. N. Darby.[93]	was
The Interlinear Bible. (The Interlinear English Version.)[94]	was
The Living Bible.[95]	was
The New English Bible.[96]	was
The New International Version.[97]	was
The New JPS. Version Of The Tanakh.[98]	being
The Revised Standard Version.[99]	was
The Revised Version.[100]	was

Of the twenty-three versions listed above, only two, that is just under 9%, use *became*. The other 91% use; *being* (found twice), or *was* (found on 19 occasions). Now, of course there are instances where majority opinion is wrong; nonetheless,

[93] *The 'Holy Scriptures' A New Translation From The Original Languages*, translated Darby, London, Stow Hill Bible And Tract Depot, 1946.

[94] Op.cit.

[95] *The Living Bible: Paraphrased*, Minneapolis, U.S.A., World Wide Publications, 1971.

[96] *The New English Bible*, Oxford, The University Press, 1970.

[97] *The Holy Bible: New International Version*, London, Hodder & Stoughton, 1979.

[98] *Tanakh: A New Translation Of The Holy According To The Traditional Hebrew Text*, Philadelphia, The Jewish Publication Society, 1985.

[99] *The Holy Bible: Revised Standard Version*, London, Collins, 1971.

[100] *The Holy Bible: Revised Version*, Oxford, The University Press, 1928.

whenever majority opinion is held to be incorrect, the onus of providing evidence most certainly lies with the challenger. Gap Theorists have no such evidence to offer I believe, as will now be revealed.

היתה as a Copula

Unless we are dealing with an exclamation, or a command; such as 'What?' or 'Stop!' every sentence comprises a subject, and a predicate, that is, a statement made about the subject. In the sentence found in Genesis 1:2a,

"And the earth was without form and void...,"

the earth is of course the subject, while, *without form and void*, is the predicate. In English, the connection between subject and predicate is made by the English word *was*, the third person singular past tense of the verb *to be*, which acts as a copula, that is, it joins or couples the subject and predicate together. The question is now, is *hayetha*, היתה, the Hebrew copula?

It is true to say that Hebrew does not always require the copula.[101] Thorleif Boman in his intriguing book, *Hebrew Thought Compared With Greek*, shows particularly clearly and logically, that the copula is most definitely required in Genesis 1:2a, and that this is precisely the function of *hayetha*, היתה, in this verse.

He begins by remarking about situations where the predicate is a substantive, observing that on these occasions the noun clause reveals the *identity* of the subject and predicate, as in Hebrew thought,

---

[101] Roddy, op.cit., pp. 500–501, Boman, op.cit., pp. 35ff., Fields, op.cit., pp. 90ff.

> "the thing is its measure, its material, or its
> identity. *hammizbeah 'ets... weqirothaw 'ets*
> (Ezek 41.22): The altar (was) wood and its
> walls (were) wood."

Here, the altar and its walls are unequivocally identifiable with
the material from which they have been made. The
identification of both is achieved without the need of a copula.
Boman gives as another example the statement that, *All the
paths of the Lord are mercy and truth*, (Psalm 25:10). Here the
Psalmist declares that, the Lord's manner of dealing is
absolutely *identical* with *mercy and truth*. Boman maintains
this identification between the Subject (*the Lord*) and the
predicate (*His paths are mercy and truth*), is so precise, that it
could even be thought that this construction is tautologous,
because the predicate is intrinsic to the subject. Were the
copula to have been employed here, it would have conveyed
what Boman terms an "unreality which can be overlooked,
indeed must be overlooked."

The situation is fundamentally different however whenever the
predicate is not intrinsic to the subject. Intriguingly for us,
Boman gives as an example of this category the very text we
are examining, *and the earth was without form and void*. This
case is completely different from the two examples given
above, argues Boman, because the predicate *thohu wabhohu* is
not intrinsic to the subject, *haerets*. The subject, the earth, is
the domain of order, of complexity, of civilisation, of
humanity; thus it cannot be conceived as being identifiable
with the predicate *thohu wabhohu*. There is a gap between the
two. This is why the copula, *hayetha*, is a definite requirement
in this instance. It must bridge the conceptual gap between
subject and predicate when the predicate is not intrinsic to the
subject. The copula tells the reader, that the earth, which in the
time of the reader, is the place of order and civilisation, was
once, *thohu wabhohu*.

In English, the fundamental difference between saying, *the earth was without form and void*, and, *the altar and its walls were made of wood*, is not present in the way in which it is for the Hebrew. But if we wish to understand fully the meaning of an Hebrew text, we must acquaint ourselves as thoroughly as we may with the ways in which the Hebrew language works.[102]

Boman then goes on to show how our way of thought differs radically from that of the ancient Hebrew, which explains why sometimes in English, we need a copula where Hebrew does not. Our first thoughts focus upon the altar, its size and its shape; only afterwards do we turn to the raw material from which it has been built. But we also assume that an altar of this type could have been made instead from copper or brass. This shows that we regard the *form* and *substance* of things as distinct, and that we give priority to the *form*. For the Hebrew, to use Boman's words:

> "the material is the thing. If an altar is wooden, then it could not possibly be copper for that would result in a totally new and different altar, namely a copper one."[103]

Boman then goes on to consider those instances where a copula is required in Hebrew, one of these instances being where a former time is being designated. He writes:

> "Here and there *hayah* is necessary to designate 'time', e.g. the earth was (*hayetha*) once upon a time waste and void, i.e. chaos (Gen 1.2); *hayethah* could not be omitted for that would give the impossible meaning that the area of civilisation was identical with chaos. Again,

---

[102] Boman, op.cit., p. 36.

[103] Ibid., pp. 36f.

> Nineveh was (once upon a time) an exceedingly great city (Jonah 3:3); to complete the sentence it is necessary to say that Nineveh is no more. Or again, Joseph was (already) in Egypt (Ex 1.5). The same use of *hayah* is surely to be found in: they were both naked (grown people no longer appear naked) (Gen 2.25). Or, the serpent was more subtle than all the other beasts of the field (Gen 3.1; cf. Gesenius–Kautzsch, 141, i), i.e. it is no longer so prudent as it was at that time. Likewise, the whole earth (humanity) had (once upon a time) one language (Gen 11.1)."[104]

Now, if the Gap Theorists are correct, then in the examples above we would have to read, *they* (Adam and Eve) *became naked*, and *the serpent became more subtle than all the other beasts of the field*, and finally, *the whole earth became to have one language*. These renditions are plainly at variance with the meaning of the texts, and provide clear examples of how wrong it would be to translate Genesis 1:2a, *And the earth became without form and void*. We have already noted that other grammatical considerations exclude this translation, but now we see how absurd a *consistent* application of the Gap Theorists' views really is.

John 1:1

In the examples above we see that *hayetha*, היתה, has been used as a copula to emphasise a condition which existed formerly, but which would seem very surprising to later generations. It is as if the writer using *hayetha*, היתה, is saying, (*in spite of what you might think from what you see*

---

around you now), there was a time when people were naked/spoke only one language/the serpent was incredibly subtle/the earth was without form and void. Doctor A. J. Roddy applies this type of reasoning to the Hebrew translation of John 1:1 and produces some interesting results. I give two examples of John 1:1 translated into Hebrew below, the English translation in the second example, is my own.[105]

היה	והדבר	הדבר	היה	בראשית
was	and the Word	the Word,	was	In (the) beginning

הרבר	היה	ואלהים	האלהים	את
the Word.	was	and God	God,	(with)

היה	והדבר	הדבר	היה	בראשית
was	and the Word	the Word,	was	In (the) beginning

הרבר	היה	ואלהים	האלהים	אצל
the Word.	was	and God	God,	with

Doctor Roddy begins by referring to the extremely close parallels between John 1:1 and Genesis 1:1–2, and then says:

> "If Gen 1:2 must be rendered "became" (after 1:1) or had become (prior to Gen 1:1) waste and void, then John 1:1b must be rendered "And the Word had become God." As though the Godhood of the Word were attained by some spiritual progression rather than being

---

[105] The first is from *The New Testament In Hebrew And English*, Edgware, Middlesex, The Society For Distributing The Holy Scriptures To The Jews, undated, the second is from ספרי הברית החדשה, Jerusalem, The United Bible Societies, 1979.

inherently His by right of being God."
(Emphases original)[106]

This is extremely compelling evidence for the normal translation, *was*, that is consistent with every other aspect of the grammar of Genesis 1:1–2. Taking Boman's lead here, I believe we now see the full force of John's statement in 1:1 of his Gospel. It is as if he were saying,

> *"In spite of what you might think of Christ, His Life did not begin when He was born of Mary, but He was in the Beginning; in spite of Him being God-with-us, He was within the Godhead from eternity; in spite of Him being really and truly man; nonetheless, He was God."*

From all of this we see that it is impossible theologically, as well as being impossible exegetically and grammatically for *hayetha*, היתה, to be translated as *became*; it may only be *was*.

Conclusion 6. היתה in Genesis 1:2 must be translated as *was*.

התו ובהו Part C

The Process of Separation after Initial Creation

There is very little controversy about how these two words, which form yet another alliteration, are to be translated. The controversy, instead, focuses on the assertion made by Gap Theorists, that it is inconceivable that God would have created the earth originally *without form and void*, and, therefore, they

---

[106] Op.cit., pp. 502–503.

say, inevitably this condition must have been the consequence of a catastrophe of some kind. The process of separation of light from darkness, the waters above, from the waters below, the dry-land from the seas, and so on, of the hexameron are viewed of course, merely as a *restorative* work. Gap Theorists view Jeremiah 4:23 as a confirmation of their beliefs, as we find the very same Hebrew expression there, in a context which is undoubtedly judgmental. Thus, it is held that the statement in Genesis 1:2 must also be understood within a context of divine judgement.

This idea however, is overturned by the consideration of the creation of man, in which a process of internal separation, similar to those which characterise the hexameron, occurs after his initial creation in Genesis 1, and results in the bringing forth of the woman, who thereafter is distinguished from the man. We notice firstly however, that prior to this act of internal separation, the man had not been the subject of any kind of rebellion, fall, or judgement, but remained in a state of pristine righteousness, which permitted full and fearless communion with God. This reveals that there is nothing intrinsically impossible about the thought of the earth being created originally in a formless and empty state, only to be given both form and population within days. The making of woman then, challenges a basic assumption of Gap Theorists, that is all the more telling for it emanating from the same overall context of creation.

How is התו ובהו to be understood?

Now while there may be little controversy as to how *thohu wabhohu*, התו ובהו, is to be translated, we do need to examine whether or not the claim of the Gap Theorist which asserts that the phrase is only ever used within a context of Divine judgement is correct. *Bhohu*, בהו, is only ever used on two other occasions, and in both of these cases it is used alongside *thohu*, תהו. *Thohu*, תהו, is used more often, but even then it is still of rare occurrence being found on but twenty occasions, just over half of which are in the book of Isaiah. The usage of both words is shown in Appendix III. From that analysis it is clear that the basic concept of the word is that of *emptiness* or *barrenness*, meanings which are not necessarily and inevitably associated with judgement, but two texts in particular are used by Gap Theorists in an attempt to prove otherwise.

Jeremiah 4:23

This is a key text for the Gap Theorists, It reads in the *Authorized Version* as,

> "I beheld the earth, and, lo, it was without form
> and void (*thohu wabhohu*, תהו ובהו); and the
> heavens, and they had no light."

Appendix III will show that this is the only instance of *thohu*, תהו, where it is found clearly and unequivocally within a context of judgement. The following verses go on to speak of the mountains and hills vibrating, probably because of earthquake activity, and Jerusalem's inhabitants evacuating the city. What should be noted clearly however, is that the act of judgement is found in the physical overthrow of Judah's cities ("broken down at the Presence of the Lord" verse 26), and the consequent desertion of them ("the whole city shall flee" verse 29), leaving a state of *emptiness*, the normal meaning for *thohu*, תהו, as Appendix III shows. I submit therefore, that the state of being *thohu wabhohu*, תהו ובהו, is of less importance, than the fact that this state, in the prophetic vision, was arrived at from *a prior condition of normality*, revealing a *process of decline*. Thus, unlike the state of *thohu wabhohu*, תהו ובהו, of Genesis 1:2, it does not describe a *static* condition; on the contrary it is the consequence of a *process*. This process is the key; it is the process of a decline, or a reversal of the city's fortunes that forms the essence of the judgement. The state of *thohu wabhohu*, תהו ובהו, is itself perfectly neutral; *it is what induced that state* which is either positive or negative. The city is taken abruptly from a positive state of organisation, into a negative state of disorganisation. In very sharp contrast to this, the situation in Genesis 1:2, is but the primary stage which is the consequence of Absolute Creation, and is in anticipation of the impending and positive climax of perfection. Therefore the achievement of the condition of *thohu wabhohu*, תהו ובהו, is, *very strictly speaking*, not the essence of the Divine judgement in Jeremiah, so much as the complete *reversal* of the city's fortunes which lead to that state. In Genesis 1:2, the same condition is a step on an upward path to perfection, allowing no room for any hint of a judgmental element. As with so many other cases, the context shows the meaning of the word, rather than the other way around.

Isaiah 45:18

This leads naturally into the other text which contains the word *thohu*, תהו, that is used widely by Gap Theorists. It is this text which originally convinced me that the Gap Theory is true, for, on the surface, it does seem to offer very strong evidence for the theory. In the Authorised Version it reads,

> "For thus saith the Lord that created the heavens; God Himself that formed the earth and made it; He hath established it, He created it not in vain (*thohu*, תהו.) He formed it to be inhabited."

In a verse which seems emphatically to be related to the subject matter of Genesis 1:2, we read, seemingly, that God did not create the earth in a condition of *thohu*, תהו. Yet in Genesis 1:1–2 we seem to find the reverse! The Gap Theory then seems to be *required* in order to resolve the apparent difficulty. It permits both seemingly contradictory texts to be literally true.

Given this situation, when reading Arthur Custance' book *Without Form And Void* for the first time, I was particularly surprised that he made so little use of this text, and, that he seemed to regard it as being a long way short of the absolute proof for the Gap Theory that I had believed it to be. Custance even goes as far as to say that this verse is only what he calls a "strong witness" to those who *already* support the Gap Theory.[107] Why should the leading exponent of the Gap Theory have such reticence about promoting this verse as the strong evidence I believed it to be? Firstly, Custance pointed out something I had not noticed originally, namely that there is yet another instance of *thohu*, תהו, in the very next verse! This is remarkable. The word is extremely rare as we have already seen, yet it occurs twice in successive verses. Clearly there must be a connection. Many commentators over the years have shown by this, that in these verses we find an instance of Hebrew *poetic parallelism*. Doctor Roddy sets out this parallelism as below;

---

[107] Op.cit., p. 115.

"Yea, thus saith Jehovah,

> Creator of the heavens—

He is The God,

> Creator of the earth,

> Maker of Her!

He stood her upright!

> Not tohu did

> He create her!

> For dwelling did He

> Form her!

I did not say to Jacob's seed,

> Tohu

> Seek ye Me!

I am Jehovah,

Speaker of Righteousness,

Proclaimer of uprightness."[108]

The *Companion Bible*, which illustrates the structural location of every verse, passage, book and division of Scripture, shows that these two verses form a part of a larger structure which encompasses the whole passage. This is illustrated below;

---

[108] Op.cit., p. 510–511.

A. Verse 16. Idolaters. Their shame and confusion.

  B Verse 17. Israel. Saved.

   C Verse 18a. Earth. Its Formation.

    D Verse 18b. None beside Jehovah.

     E Verse. 19a. The oracles of God. Plain.

      F Verse 19b. Call to the seed of Jacob.

       G Verse 20a. The escaped nation. Called.

a. Verse 20. Idolaters. Their ignorance.

  b. Verse 21. Israel's Saviour.

   c. Verse 22a. Earth. Call to.

    d. Verse 22b. "None beside Elohim".

     e. Verse 23. The oath of God. Sure.

      f. Verses 24-24. Call to the seed of Israel.[109]

It is clear then from the structuring we see above, that we have to consider *both* occurrences of *thohu*, תהו, here, treating them as a matched pair which facilitates the operation of the structure. I am thankful that Arthur Custance was honest enough to admit this candidly. Discussing the occurrence of *thohu*, תהו, in verse 18, Custance writes:

> "The propriety of adopting the Authorized Version rendering must be admitted in the light of verse 19 which reads, "I have not spoken in secret, in a dark place of the earth: I said not unto the seed of Jacob, Seek ye Me in vain (*Tohu*)".

Certainly in verse 19 the translation is much more reasonable than it would have been had *Tohu* been rendered "a ruin", for

---

[109] Based on the structure found in *The Companion Bible*, London, The Lamp Press, undated, in.loc.

then the sentence would have read, "Seek ye Me, a ruin"—
which is nonsense. He says, shortly afterwards:

> "The sentence structure in verse 19 *forces* one
> to render the noun adverbially and thus to read
> it as "in vain". To do anything else makes
> nonsense of the sentence."

He also notes:

> "If one must render *Tohu* "in vain" in *this*
> passage, it cannot be altogether unreasonable to
> so render it in verse 18 where such a rendering
> does, after all, make very good sense."[110]

Of course Custance goes on to argue nonetheless that *thohu*,
תהו, in verse 18 should still be rendered as *a ruin*, but it is
interesting to note that he himself states correctly that it cannot
be rendered as anything but *vain* in verse 19, and says also that
in terms of the sense of the passage, and the rules of grammar,
it may also be translated as *vain* in verse 18. Now this is where
the background is so important. Custance is quite correct when
he says that in verse 18, *thohu*, תהו, might be translated either
as *ruin* or *vain*; but, crucially, it may <u>only</u> be translated as *vain*
in verse 19. But Custance ignores the crucial fact that we are
considering here a classic example of Hebrew parallelism, as
the structures show, in which thoughts and concepts reflect
one another. Thus, whatever the meaning of *thohu*, תהו, is in
one passage; it must be the same in the other. As was said
above, the parallelism of the structure forces our hand here,
thohu, תהו, must be translated *consistently*, and this leaves
only the option of rendering it as *vain* in both connected
verses, as there is no other option in verse 19. Further, the
grammatical facts already examined relating to the preceding

---

[110] Op.cit., p. 114.

words of Genesis 1:2 exclude the option of *ruin* as we saw above. Therefore consistency of exegesis, and respect for Hebrew parallelism and grammar demands that *thohu*, תהו, be translated as *vain* in *both* occurrences of the word in this passage, and the supposed proof text of the Gap Theory is seen to be as firmly opposed to it as any other we have examined so far.

Additionally, as a late close friend pointed out to me, had it been intended by the Holy Spirit to state that the Lord did not create the earth in a state of *thohu wabhohu*, תהו ובהו, it is very surprising indeed that only *thohu*, תהו, is found here, whereas, in Jeremiah 4:23, where a specific reference to Genesis 1:2 is plain to see, the entire phrase *thohu wabhohu*, תהו ובהו, is used, as we have just seen.

Finally, the rendering of *vain* is quite consistent with the basic meaning of *thohu*, תהו, as revealed in Appendix III. This basic meaning is of *emptiness*, and *vanity* is indeed a form of *emptiness*. The rendering of *ruin* however is not so consistent with the concept of *emptiness*; a ruin might be empty of course, but is not so necessarily and inevitably.

I conclude then that this passage from Isaiah shows that God neither created the earth, or requested the seed of Jacob to seek Him, in vain. Fulfilment followed both.

Conclusion 7. The phrase תהו ובהו in Genesis 1:2 refers to the initial emptiness of the earth, and does not imply a condition brought about through ruination.

Conclusion to Chapter Two

While the establishment of Genesis 1:1 as an Independent Statement, did seem to detach it from Genesis 1:2, inasmuch, as verse 1 could not be viewed as a clause dependent upon verse 2 (or 3), we have seen in this chapter that, by a striking contrast, verse 2 is dependent upon verse 1! The grammatical facts unearthed in this chapter; namely that verse 2 is an explanatory circumstantial noun clause, coupled with verse 1 by waw-copulative, reveal this unexpected result. This has the effect of course of binding together these two verses every bit as tightly as would have been the case had verse 1 been a clause dependent on verse 2 or 3, which it is not. Even the alliteration of *bereshith bara*, בראשית ברא, and *thohu wabhohu*, תהו ובהו, has its echo in the doubling of *haerets*, הארץ, at the junction of the two verses, which is effected by the conjunction waw, ו, underlining again the affinity of each verse for the other, and their inseparable state. The occurrence of *hayetha*, היתה, in verse 2 does not weaken the connection between verses 1 and 2, as it is required to fulfil the rôle of copula in verse 2, uniting subject and predicate, the latter being the famous expression, *thohu wabhohu*, תהו ובהו, *without form and void*. This phrase is plainly not necessarily and inevitably associated with judgement at all, but means simply *emptiness*. It is the realisation of these facts that has driven some to locate the gap before verse 1 as we saw. These people see with clarity the grammatical impossibility of accommodating any gap between the two verses. As we have already seen, however, the fact that verse 1 is an Independent Statement of Absolute Creation renders the placement of a gap before Genesis 1:1 just as impossible as it is to place it between verses 1 and 2. Thus our findings now exclude the possibility of a chronological gap anywhere before the hexameron!

The conclusion must be then that the text of Genesis 1:1–2 does not allow the concept of a gap either side of verse 1.

Part Two

Is there evidence of a gap from other Scripture texts?

Chapter Three

Alleged support from other Hebrew Canonical texts

The assertion that there is a gap either before Genesis 1:1, or between Genesis 1:1 and 1:2 is based partly on Scripture texts other than those just examined, however. Although it has already been shown that the basis for belief in the Gap Theory is utterly untenable, no survey of the Gap Theory may ignore the Gap Theorist's view of these other texts. In this chapter we examine those found in the Hebrew Canon; in the next, those found in the Christian Canon.

Part A: ברא and עשה

Outstanding from Chapter One is the consideration of two different ways of viewing the Hebrew words *bara*, ברא, and *asah*, עשה. We will begin our examination of the first category of texts then by addressing this issue.

ברא and עשה

Those who are opposed to the existence of a Gap before Genesis 1:1, but, nonetheless assert that there is a Gap between Genesis 1:1 and 2, frequently claim to find support for their view in the use of the Hebrew words referred to above. Such believers will very readily agree that *bara*, ברא, as used in Genesis 1:1 refers to what is popularly known as *creatio-ex-nihilo*, or, more accurately as we have seen, *ex-creation*, or, Absolute Creation from the resources of Deity alone; but then insist that *asah*, עשה, means the exact opposite; namely, creation from pre-existing material. Thus the widespread use of *asah*, עשה, in connection within the hexameron[111] is held to show that the hexameron was but *a period of restoration of the earth* from a ruinous state, rather than its initial creation, which occurred in Genesis 1:1, under the term *bara*, ברא.

It must be admitted that Parkhurst's *Hebrew Lexicon* might seem to give some support for this view, as it gives the primary meaning of *asah*, עשה, in the opening words of its definition as, "To make out of pre-existent matter."[112] Two things should caution the student here however. Firstly, *bara*, ברא, itself may refer to *cutting* or *carving* out of raw-material when it is not in Qal as we saw above, and even when it is in Qal, the phenomenon of Absolute Creation is revealed simply by the universal absence of any accusative of material, the fact that Deity is the Subject exclusively, and that the subject-context, and syntax reveal the absence of raw-material, rather than the essential meaning of the word. Secondly, creation without raw-material, being the prerogative of Deity alone is so conspicuously rare, that it is wholly unreasonable to suppose that any word in any language is reserved exclusively for the concept. To recall Robert Young's comments:

> "To create from nothing is a phrase, and no language on earth, it is believed, can express it, save by a phrase."[113]

---

[111] See Appendix IV.

[112] Parkhurst, John, *An Hebrew And Chaldee Lexicon Without Points*, London, 1813, in.loc.

[113] Op.cit., p. 1.

It is vital then that the context be examined carefully and prayerfully before dogmatic statements about the usage of *asah*, עשׂה, are made. A reference to Davidson's *Analytical Lexicon*,[114] and Gesenius' *Lexicon*,[115] as well as Wigram's *Englishman's Hebrew Lexicon*[116] will reveal how enormously wide is the scope of this word, showing the truth of Robert Young's observation, that it "has a great latitude of meaning and application."[117]

The Sun and Moon

Pember,[118] Custance,[119] and even the *New Scofield Reference Bible*[120] all seek to illustrate how *asah*, עשׂה, does not mean *create*, from the events of Day Four of the hexameron. Here, we learn of the creation of the sun and the moon. The argument is that as plant life had been created on Day Three, the light and heat of the sun would be required at that point to allow the flora to survive. Thus, Day Four, it is said, saw only the *appointment* of the pre-existing sun and moon, rather than their actual creation, which must have been in *The Beginning* of Genesis 1:1. *The New Scofield Reference Bible* offers the following scheme to harmonise the account in Genesis 1 with the wisdom of man:

---

[114] Op.cit., in.loc.

[115] Op.cit., in.loc.

[116] Wigram, George V., *The Englishman's Hebrew And Chaldee Concordance Of The Old Testament*, Grand Rapids, Michigan, U.S.A., Zondervan, 1970, based on Bagster's editions of 1843, & 1860, in.loc.

[117] Op.cit., p. 2.

[118] Op.cit., pp. 91f.

[119] Op.cit., pp. 178ff.

[120] *The New Scofield Reference Bible*, edited Scofield, & Schuyler, Oxford University Press, 1967, in.loc.

> "Neither here [verse 3] nor in vv. 14–18 is an original creative act implied. A different word [*asah*, עשה] is used. The sense is *made to appear, made visible*. The sun and moon were created "in the beginning." The light came from the sun, of course, but the vapour diffused the light. Later the sun appeared in an unclouded sky [The words in square brackets are my own]."[121]

This, for a believer is completely untenable. If by the words

> "And God made two great lights... and God set them in the firmament of the heaven" (verses 15–17)

we are actually supposed to understand instead,

> "And God lifted the fog so that the pre-existing sun might be made visible,"

then it is vitally important that we are told *why* the text does not speak about the lifting of a fog revealing a pre-existent sun, when it might have done, rather than the creation of the sun and the moon! This meaning is very far indeed from how the words of the text would be understood ordinarily. All in all, this is a most remarkable statement for any believer to make.

To presume that no plant life could survive without the sun and moon however is to assume that light and heat may only reach the soil that contained the plant-life of Day Three from the sun. This belief, based upon human reasoning and experience, ignores the clear statement of the Apocalypse, where, in the New Heavens and the New Earth, we find

---

[121] Ibid.

abundant plant life flourishing without the presence of any sun to provide either light or warmth. Both are given lavishly and directly through the Presence of God (Revelation 22:1–5).[122] Now, in Genesis 1:2 we are told that The Spirit Of God was moving over the face of the waters, the context making clear that this action facilitated the creative acts of the hexameron. Every true believer will understand, that the Infinite resources of The Holy Spirit are easily sufficient to provide directly, without the aid of nature, whatever environment was needed to induce growth.

It is of interest to note that the view expressed in *The New Scofield Reference Bible* has an extremely long history. In the somewhat dreary Babylonian account of the creation, the sun and the moon are merely appointed on Day Four, because they were conceived by the Babylonians to be gods.[123] Thus, as gods, they could not have been created, but were thought to be eternal like the creator.

The account in Genesis 1 militates firmly against this pagan concept embraced by the Babylonian view by showing that light and heat are older than the sun, and derive from the Godhead. It shows also, and just as importantly, that, as the Lord directly breathed the breath of lives into Adam (Genesis 2:7), so too, the light and warmth needed for plant growth were provided directly by the Lord, as will be the case

---

[122] Given the very many parallels between the Apocalypse and the book of Genesis, this illustration is probably of particular significance. See Bullinger, E. W., *The Apocalypse Or "The Day Of The Lord,"* London, Eyre & Spottiswoode, 1935, pp. 57ff. Cf. also I John 1:5, "God is light, and in Him is no darkness at all," and Revelation 1:16, cf. Colossians 1:16.

[123] See Sayce, A. H., *Monument Facts And Higher Critical Fancies*, London, The Religious Tract Society, 1904, pp. 99–100, & *The "Higher Criticism" And The Verdict Of The Monuments*, London, The Society For Promoting Christian Knowledge, 1915, pp. 61ff.

in the New Heavens and New Earth. The truth about
ex-creation that we saw above, of course, should make this
suggestion quite acceptable. Again, just as Adam was able to
breathe normally after his creation, so too the sun is able to
provide us with light and heat through its own natural activity,
but we see from Genesis that breath *predates* man, and heat
and light *predate* the sun. It is interesting to notice that this
situation emphasises the position of subservience to, and
dependence upon the creator of the two things within creation
that mankind is most inclined to worship; the host of heaven,
and himself. This state of subservience and dependency of the
two great foci of man's idolatry is obscured by the proponents
of the Gap Theory I submit.

The structure of Genesis 1 should also be noted. In the first
three days, *static conditions* or environments are created which
are incapable of movement. This is why plants appear in this
cycle, although, because of the principle of life that they
possess, they represent the climax of this first cycle,
nonetheless, in common with everything else in the cycle, they
are incapable of independent movement. All that is found in
the second cycle of the final three days is *dynamic*. The sun,
moon and stars reveal movement within the heavens, marine
and winged life created on Day Five move by swimming and
flying, while the animals, and man, move by walking, jumping
or running. All that is found in the second cycle of three days is
dynamic within its corresponding *static* environment of the first
cycle of three days. (This consideration shows incidentally, that
the unformed and unfilled condition of the earth, described as
thohu wabhohu, תהו ובהו, must be a *static* condition, rather
than the consequence of a process, as the grammar requires in
order to fit in with this very clear pattern.)

I see no reason at all then to disbelieve the plain reading of
Genesis 1:14–18 which speaks of the creation of the sun and
the moon on Day Four, and, therefore no need at all to believe
that *asah*, עשה, here, does not mean, *create*. If we press on,

however, we will uncover definite reasons for believing that the scope of the word *asah*, עשה, does indeed include Absolute Creation.

The views of Pember and Custance are untenable

In Exodus 20:11 and 31:17 we read that,

> "in six days the Lord made heaven and earth."

In both of these texts the Hebrew word translated *made*, is *asah*, עשה.[124] Pember and Custance both insist that this work was a restorative work, and that the usage of *asah*, עשה, indicates as much. Custance writes:

> "It is very frequently argued that the wording of Exod 20.11, "For in six days the Lord made heaven and earth, the sea, and all that in them is, and rested on the seventh day...," excludes the possibility of a gap between Gen 1.1 and 1.2 because the whole process of creation was completed within these six days... What we are told here is that God in six days "made" (עשה *asah*) the heaven and the earth. It does not say that He created (ברא *bara*) them in six days."[125]

Custance then goes on to discuss how *asah*, עשה, means *appoint* as well as *make*, and that this means that Exodus 20:11, (and, therefore 31:17 as well) could easily refer to a restoration of the earth after its ruination.

This view that is a fundamental part of the Gap Theorist's argument, and is surprisingly widespread, is completely

---

[124] *The Interlinear Bible: Hebrew–Greek–English*, edited and translated Green, Peabody, Massachusetts, U.S.A., Hendrickson, second edition 1986, in.loc.

[125] Op.cit., p. 178.

invalid I believe. We have already seen that *bara*, בְּרָא, has a very *narrow* range of meaning, and that, by contrast, *asah*, עָשָׂה, has a very *broad* scope of meaning. Now within the hexameron *bara*, בְּרָא, occurs on four different occasions, all of which are in Qal, which means that definite acts of Absolute Creation are referred to within the six days of Exodus 20:11 and 31:17. These acts of Absolute Creation include the creation of all types of marine life, as well as human life. By comparing Genesis 1 with Exodus 20:11, and 31:17 then, it would seem that every act of Absolute Creation (*bara*, בְּרָא), recorded in Genesis 1, constitutes something that was made (*asah*, עָשָׂה), in the texts in Exodus, but not everything that was made (*asah*, עָשָׂה), was an Absolute Creation (*bara*, בְּרָא).

Further, we notice too from Genesis 1:26–27 that man was first _made_ (*asah*, עָשָׂה), and then _created_ (*bara*, בְּרָא). Now this confounds the views of Custance and his followers emphatically, for, if they are right, man was restored, *before* he was originally created! An obvious impossibility.

Additionally, Nehemiah 9:6 reads,

> "Thou hast made (*asah*, עָשָׂה) heaven, the heaven of heavens, with all their host, the earth, and all things that are therein, the seas, and all that is therein."

Here, not just the heaven and earth, as in the texts in Exodus, which could be explained away as just the earth and the firmament of heaven of Genesis 1:6–8, but the _heaven of heavens_ are said to have been made (*asah*, עָשָׂה). But this phrase, *the heaven of heavens*, inevitably takes us back to the creation of Genesis 1:1, as only the firmament of heaven is referred to in the hexameron. Genesis 1:2 Gap Theorists agree that the creation of the heavens in Genesis 1:1 was an act of Absolute Creation (*bara*, בְּרָא), nevertheless, we see here it is embraced within the scope of *asah*, עָשָׂה.

Remembering the narrowness of scope of *bara*, בְּרָא, and the contrasting breadth of scope of *asah*, עָשָׂה, we see that what the texts of Exodus 20:11 and 31:17, and Nehemiah 9:6 show is that an act of Absolute Creation (*bara*, בָּרָא) is always an act of *making* or *producing* something (*asah*, עָשָׂה). From Gesenius' Lexicon it seems apparent that the essential meaning of *asah*, עָשָׂה, is *activity* (in making something). This activity may be, but is not necessarily or inevitably, Divine. However, when it relates to an act of Absolute Creation (*bara*, בָּרָא in Qal), then the activity certainly is Divine. We see that *activity in making or producing* is the essential meaning of *asah*, עָשָׂה, clearly when we come to the account of the institution of the Sabbath Rest. Here the context is a *cessation of activity*, which gives place to restfulness. The pattern offered to Adam, is that of God disengaging from His creative activity, setting the example for Adam. The activity God is said to have rested from is *asah*, עָשָׂה. This is why *asah*, עָשָׂה, is found in the texts referred to in Exodus 20:11 and 31:17. *They are both clear references to the establishment of the Sabbath Rest*, and must utilise the contrast between rest and activity which the usage of *asah*, עָשָׂה, provides.

In references to acts of *making or producing* by God, the emphasis is upon the *activity* of Deity; in references to acts of Absolute Creation, the emphasis is upon the uniqueness of the act itself, its unexpectedness, and special spiritual significance. What is in focus then is the act itself, rather than the exertion required to produce it. This is why it may be said of man that he was *made* before he was *created*. The first word shows the direct *activity* of Deity; the second word concentrates upon the uniqueness, unexpectedness, and spiritual significance of this particular act. (The word *form*, *yahtsar*, יָצַר, I propose refers to the *process*).

A definite clue to this is the fact that *breeth*, ברית, the Hebrew word for *Covenant* is related closely with *bara*, ברא.[126] The most well known Scriptural Covenant, that of circumcision involves a *cutting* (the basic meaning of *bara*, ברא, as we saw) of the flesh of course, and even today we talk of *cutting a deal*, which is a very distant echo of the association between *cutting* and *covenant*. A Covenant necessarily involves activity, but the activity is not what is spiritually significant. The spiritual value of the Covenant is in the unique and significant relationship between the Covenant parties that is established, rather than the labour required in enacting it.

One text in particular shows these complimentary, but different meanings of *bara*, ברא, and *asah*, עשה. In Genesis 2:3, we find ברא אלהים לעשות, which means, following Gesenius, *God produced (or created) by making*. That is, God had, through His Own constructive activity, Created Absolutely. As this phrase occurs in the passage which summarises the work of the hexameron, and is explanatory of the establishment of the Sabbath rest, we see that every act of Absolute Creation of the hexameron was achieved through the productive activity of the Godhead. The concept of the hexameron being a period of restoration collapses in the light of this verse.

Conclusion 8. עשה certainly does not only mean *restore*. When it is used in a context of creation by God, it shows that what is created is the consequence of Divine activity. Hence every act of Absolute Creation, ברא, is an act of עשה.

Conclusion 9. It follows from this that עשה and ברא are not synonyms, as is often claimed by opponents of the Gap Theory. They are entirely different words, one of which is very narrow in its scope, while the other is correspondingly broad in scope.

---

[126] See Gesenius, op.cit., in.loc.

Before moving on to the next Part of this chapter, there is one more consideration concerning this passage of Scripture. It is sometimes believed that the English word *replenish* in Genesis 1:28, implies that this was a command to refill the earth after a catastrophic ruination within the alleged gap. The Hebrew verb *mahlah*, מלא, really means only *fill*, not re-fill, a fact which even Arthur Custance readily acknowledges.[127]

Conclusion 10. The command of Genesis 1:28, is a command to *fill* the earth; not to re-fill it after a ruination which occurred in a supposed gap before the hexameron.

Part B: Other Texts

The next text to examine is Genesis 2:4:

> "These are the generations of the heavens and of
> the earth when they were created, *in the day* that
> the Lord God made the earth and the heavens."

Gap Theorists point out that on none of the six days may it be said that the Lord God made the earth and the heavens; they were created in Genesis 1:1 before the hexameron began. It is thought to follow from this, there must have been days which antedate the hexameron, indicating the presence of a Gap between Genesis 1:1 and 2 therefore.

Genesis 2:4 as a Colophon

Superficially, this seems to suggest that there might indeed be a period of time before the hexameron, but this is not the case.

---

[127] Op.cit., p. 8.

I have shown in *The Inspiration Of The Pentateuch*,[128] that the first thirty-six chapters of Genesis derive from texts written originally on clay tablets which end with a literary device known as a colophon which records the nature of the history written on the tablet or series of tablets, sometimes the time of writing and the name of the author, and, very significantly, the *title* of the work. Understanding these crucial facts reveals that Genesis 2:4, *These are the generations of the heavens and of the earth when they were created, in the day that the Lord God made the earth and the heavens*, is the title of the previous section which begins at Genesis 1:1. It is an interesting and relevant fact that our title for the first book of the Bible; *Genesis*, derives from the Septuagint, 'Γενεσις', a word which was taken from the word 'generations' in this very verse, because the translators of the Septuagint realised that Genesis 2:4 was the title of the initial section of the book. As the Septuagint was compiled in the Third Century B.C.E., the translators were more thoroughly acquainted with the literary practices of antiquity than, generally speaking, we are today. Cuneiform scholars are well aware of the nature and function of these colophons, and many examples may be found in works which refer to the discovery of ancient cuneiform texts.[129]

Now the final colophon to be found within the Pentateuch is at Numbers 3:1 which also contains the phrase "in the day." *These are the histories of Aaron and Moses in the day that the Lord spake with Moses in Mount Sinai*. Now we know clearly from the narrative that there were very many days in which the

---

[128] Phelan, M. W. J., *The Inspiration Of The Pentateuch*, Waterlooville, Twoedged Sword Publications, 2005, Cap. VIII.

[129] See Hooker, J. T., *Reading The Past*, London, British Museum Publications, 1990, and Parrot, A., *The Flood And Noah's Ark*, translated Hudson, London, SCM Press, 1955, pp. 32ff, and Wiseman, P. J., *New Discoveries In Babylonia About Genesis,* London, Marshall, Morgan And Scott, seventh edition, 1958, pp. 63ff.

Lord spoke to Moses in Mount Sinai, not merely one. Hebrew scholars have long recognised in this phrase a Hebrew idiom, and often translate the phrase, *in the day*, by *at the time of*, or, *when*. One example is to be found in the new Jewish Publication Society's translation of the Tanakh, or the Hebrew Canon. This reads at Numbers 3:1, <u>*At the time*</u> *that the Lord spoke with Moses on Mount Sinai*. The same version translates Genesis 2:4 as *Such is the story of the heaven and earth* <u>*when*</u> *they were created.*[130]

As was said above, we must remember that Genesis 2:4 is colophonic, that is, it actually gives the subject of the preceding narrative. The Jewish commentator, Nahum Sarna, who is well aware of this, and advocates that the phrase "in the day" in Genesis 2:4 should be understood as meaning simply *when*, points out that the Babylonian creation epic the *Enuma Elish* describes the time of the creation in a similar manner, and he adds that *enuma*, a part of the title, actually means *when*. A colophon, as was said above, gives the name or titles of the text it is appended to.

Conclusion 11. From all of this, it would appear that the phrase "in the day" in Genesis 2:4 is a Hebrew idiom for *when*, and is not a reference to one particular day, and, therefore, cannot designate a day before the hexameron.

Plant life before the hexameron?

Again in Genesis chapter 2, the translation of verses 4–5 as they are in The Authorized Version has seemed to some to indicate that plants which now grow in the earth, existed before the hexameron. The Authorized Version reads beginning at the end of verse 4:

---

[130] Op.cit., p. 5, see also Driver, S. R., *The Book Of Genesis*, London, Methuen & Co., fourth edition, 1905, p. 37.

"in the day that the Lord God made the earth
and the heavens, and every plant of the field
before it was in the earth, and every herb of the
field before it grew."

By contrast, Rotherham, in his *Emphasised Bible* translated
this passage thus,

"Now no bush of the field as yet was in the earth,
and no herb of the field as yet had sprung up."[131]

Robert Young offers,

"and no shrub of the field is yet in the earth, and
no herb of the field yet sprouteth."[132]

J. N. Darby, in a footnote to his translation offers,

"no shrub [of the field] was yet in the earth and
no herb [of the field] had yet grown."[133]

Jay P. Green renders it thus,

"and every shrub of the field was not yet on the
earth, and every plant of the field had not yet
sprung up."[134]

In similar vein, Keil and Delitzsch in their commentary have,

---

[131] *The Emphasised Bible*, op.cit., in.loc.

[132] *Literal Translation Of The Holy Bible*, translated by Young, R., Grand
Rapids, Michigan, Baker Books, 2000, in.loc.

[133] *The 'Holy Scriptures': A New Translation From The Original
Languages*, translated Darby, J. N., London, Stow Hill Bible And Tract
Depot, 1970, in.loc. I have given in square brackets, the words Darby
omitted in his footnote through want of space.

[134] *A Literal Translation Of The Bible, being a part of The Interlinear
Bible: Hebrew–English–Greek*, edited and translated Green, Jay P.,
op.cit., in.loc.

> "And as yet there was (arose, grew) no shrub of
> the field upon the earth, and no herb of the field
> sprouted; for Jehovah Elohim had not caused it
> to rain upon the earth, and there was no man to
> till the ground."

They go on to explain that these words do not relate to the
initial creation of plant life, but instead relate only to the
planting of the garden of Eden. They urge that the cultivation
of the herbs and shrubs is to be distinguished from the initial
creation of the vegetable Kingdom, and pertains to their
development within Eden. This was to be achieved through
the provision of water and the work of Adam, unlike the initial
creation which was dependent upon God alone. They add that
the shrub and herb of the field represent only a certain
category of plants, and that the term *the field* (*Sahdch*, שׂדה)
designates, not the entire planet, but only arable land suitable
for horticulture. Similarly, the *beast of the field* of 2:19
and 3:1 is to be distinguished from the *beast of the earth* of
1:24–25, as the former relates only to animals that live upon
the field and its produce. By contrast, the term *beast of the
earth* refers to all wild animals. Again, the terms, *shrub of the
field* and, *herb of the field*, relate to those trees that are
cultivated for their fruit, and the seed producing plants that
provide us with cereal crops, and other edible vegetables.[135]

Conclusion 12. Genesis 2:5 must not be understood as
indicating that plant life preceded the hexameron.

The Fall of Lucifer

In Ezekiel 28:12–19 there is a very well-known passage
which, under the surface-story of the lamentation upon the

---

[135] Op.cit., in.loc.

King of Tyre, is actually an account of the Fall of Lucifer. The relevance for us is that in verses 13–14 of the passage we read:

> "Thou hast been in Eden the Garden of God; every precious stone was thy covering, the sardius, topaz, and the diamond, the beryl, the onyx, and the jasper, the sapphire, the emerald, and the carbuncle, and gold: the workmanship of thy tabrets and of thy pipes was prepared in thee in the day that thou wast created. Thou art the Anointed Cherub that covereth; and I have set thee so: thou wast upon the holy mountain of God; thou hast walked up and down in the midst of the stones of fire."

Undoubtedly, here we have left the King of Tyre far behind and are dealing with another king who had been in Eden, and who was of a most dazzling appearance.

According to many Gap Theorists the Eden that was visited by this stunningly beautiful creature cannot be the Eden of Genesis 2–3, as it is a place whose beauty derives from spectacular minerals and exotic fire, rather than that of a well-watered garden. The existence of another Eden, so the argument goes, proves the existence of a time before the Eden we read of in Genesis, and, therefore is indicative of a Gap before the hexameron.[136]

Firstly, it must be pointed out that, as there is a *Jerusalem Above*, that is, the heavenly Jerusalem (Galatians 4:16, Hebrews 12:22, Revelation 3:12, 21:2, 10.), which exists independently of, yet simultaneously with, the Jerusalem-which-now-is, (or *Jerusalem-Below*) (Galatians 4:25), so, there might well be an heavenly Eden too. Furthermore, if

---

[136] See, Whitcomb, J. C., Jr., who though opposed to this view, refers to it in *The Early Earth*, London, Evangelical Press, 1972, p. 130.

we examine the making of the ark of the covenant, and the tabernacle, we find that Moses was under the most explicit instructions to ensure it was produced according to patterns that had been revealed to him (Exodus 25:9, 40; Numbers 8:4). We see that within the heavens there is a Temple (Hebrews 9, and Revelation 3:12; 7:15; 11:1–19; 14:15–17; 15:5-8; 16:1,17), and altar (Revelation 6:9; 8:3–5; 9:13; 11:1; 14:18; 16:7), and an ark (Revelation 11:19), and that these would seem to be the patterns from which the earthly Tabernacle, Temple, and Ark derive. Their genuine existence however, does not make any less real, the ark and Tabernacle associated with Moses; thus, *even if it could be proved by Gap Theorists that Lucifer visited another Eden*, by no means does it mean what Gap Theorists maintain, as it could have been an heavenly Eden, from which the garden planted in Genesis 2 takes its name. But, besides this, we see that the stones of fire are located in *the mountain of God*, which might be a location altogether different from the Eden, (celestial or terrestrial) of Ezekiel 28:13. I feel Gap Theorists have made far too much of this passage, and do so, simply because they lack any other scriptures to support their views.

Conclusion 13. The possible reference to another Eden in Ezekiel 28, does not indicate a history prior to the hexameron, as this conjectured other Eden is likely to be located within the heavens. Thus, Lucifer might easily have been in this heavenly Eden, within the time-scale required by a 'non-gap' understanding of the opening chapters of Genesis, before descending to the earthly Eden to meet with Eve.

Job

Similarly, it is sometimes said that the passage in Job 9:5–10 is an allusion to the destruction of the pre-hexameron world,[137]

---

[137] Pember, op.cit., pp. 82–83.

but there is no real evidence that this is so, beyond the strength of the Gap Theorists' assertion. There might be difficulties associated with locating the incidents referred to in this passage, but that does not compel acceptance of the Gap Theory, or belief in an alleged catastrophic judgement upon a pre-Adamic world.

Summary

None of the texts listed above comprises evidence for the Gap Theory, and, ironically, the consideration of *asah*, עשׂה, and *bara*, ברא, actually militates <u>*against*</u> the Gap Theory.

Chapter Four

Alleged support from the Christian Canon

In this chapter we examine the supplementary arguments used by Gap Theorists that relate to texts found in the Christian Canon. The first of these concerns the phrase *The Foundation Of The World*, and perhaps comprises the most significant support Gap Theorists claim to find in the New Testament.

Part A: The foundation of the world

This phrase is found in the Christian Canon on ten occasions which are set out below;

Matthew 13:35.	John 17:24.	Hebrews 9:26.	Revelation 17:8.
Matthew 25:34.	Ephesians 1:4.	I Peter 1:20.	
Luke 11:50.	Hebrews 4:3.	Revelation 13:8.	

In each of these occasions, the phrase in Greek is καταβολης κοσμου. The claim made by Gap Theorists is that this phrase does not mean, *the foundation of the world*, but the <u>overthrow</u> *of the earth*, or *the <u>overthrow</u> of the cosmos*. This then is claimed to be a direct reference to the ruination of the earth during the supposed gap before Genesis 1:2, and which caused the earth to be in the condition of *thohu wabhohu*, תהו ובהו, immediately before the hexameron.[138]

This belief is based upon the construction of the word καταβολης, which is an amalgam of κατα (down) and βολ (throw) and means literally *down-throwing*, or the *laying-down* of some object.[139] This negative, destructive, connotation of an act of demolition by *throwing down*, does seem often to apply to the associated verb καταβαλλω, and seems convincing enough, until we find out how the <u>noun</u> καταβολης is actually used within Scripture. On the only occasion of its use in the Christian Canon not listed in the table above, it clearly does not mean *overthrow* at all, quite the opposite in fact. This only other occasion is Hebrews 11:11 where we read,

> "Through faith... Sara herself received strength to *conceive* (καταβολην) seed."

It is completely out of the question to understand καταβολην in any negative way at all in this passage. Far from this text talking about the *ruination* or *overthrow* of the seed of Abraham, it concerns the faithfulness of God in *establishing* that seed! Gap Theorists must take notice of this text which speaks of what we might call *the foundation* of the seed of Abraham, relating to the precise moment that the line of his seed began.

There are no other occurrences of καταβολης in the Christian Canon, nor does it occur in the Greek translation of the

---

[138] Custance, op.cit., pp. 175–177.

[139] Schaefer, R. H., in the article *Before The Foundation Of The World*, in *Scripture Research*, Volume II, Number 16, Atascadero, California, Ewalt Memorial Bible School, pp. 518–519.

Hebrew Canon, but it does occur in the Apocrypha, in II Maccabees 2:29,[140] where we read,

"For as the *Master-Builder* of a new house…"

The Greek word for Master-Builder, is καταβολης, and, again, certainly cannot be understood in a negative way as signifying *demolition, ruination* or *overthrow*, but must be understood in a positive manner, namely, that of establishment.[141]

Liddell and Scott in their famous lexicon, which draws upon Greek classical literature, as well as Scripture and Christian writings, show how the verb καταβαλλω does indeed often mean to *overthrow*, but when the noun καταβολη is considered, they give under their second heading the meaning of a *foundation* or *beginning*, citing the reference in Ephesians 1:4 as an example of the application of this meaning.[142] Arndt and Gingrich, who consider only Christian literature including the Scriptures, agree with this, but give these two definitions as the *primary* meaning of the noun.[143] Abbott-Smith gives only two definitions of the noun, 1) the event leading to conception, and 2) a foundation (of a house). He then lists the texts given in the table above under this second heading.[144]

From the lexical evidence it seems clear that the phrase *Foundation Of The World*, is perfectly legitimate, and far from meaning in its Scriptural usages the *demolition, ruination* or

---

[140] E. Hatch, and H. A. Redpath, *A Concordance To The Septuagint*, Grand Rapids, Michigan, Baker Books, 1998, in.loc.

[141] *The Septuagint With Apocrypha: Greek And English*, op.cit., in.loc.

[142] Liddell and Scott, *Greek-English Lexicon*, Oxford, The University Press, undated, in.loc.

[143] Op.cit., in.loc.

[144] Op.cit., in.loc.

overthrow of the world, means its *beginning*, suggesting the *laying-down* of a building's foundations.

Conclusion 14. It is a fact that on the only occasion where the noun καταβολην is used in Scripture independently of the phrase, *the foundation of the world*, it is used indisputably in a constructive context, not a destructive context. This is also the case for the only occurrence of the word in the Apocrypha. It is also of importance to note that both occasions relate to the creation of something *new*; the *beginning* of the Abrahamic Line, and the building of a *new* house. It follows from this that its usage to mark in a positive, constructive manner, the *beginning* of the heavens and the earth is a mark of great consistency.

Part B: Other Texts

II Corinthians 4:6

This verse reads in The Authorized Version:

> "For God, Who commanded the light to shine out of darkness, hath shined in our hearts, to give the light of the knowledge of the glory of God, in the face of Jesus Christ."

From this text, Gap Theorists occasionally say that it is clear that the darkness that preceded the creation of light on the first day was evil in some way, and, therefore, indicates that a Fall and Divine Judgement must have occurred prior to the first day of the hexameron.[145]

---

[145] Custance, op.cit., pp. 15–16.

This seems to me to be an instance where a very great deal is built upon but a slight foundation. Crucially, the darkness of the first day is actually *named* by God, ("…and the darkness He called Night"). It is not credible to suppose that that which was specifically named by God, an act which implies Lordship over that which is named, (cf. Genesis 2:20, with 1:26), would not be included in the remarks found in Genesis 1:31:

> "And God saw every thing that He had made, and behold, it was very good."

Conclusion 15. The darkness of Genesis 1 was not evil.

Hebrews 11:3

In The Authorised Version this text reads:

> "The worlds were framed by the Word of God."

The claim made here by Gap Theorists is that the Greek word translated as *framed*, κατηρτισθαι, a form of καταρτιζω (perfect tense, passive voice, infinitive mood),[146] actually means *repaired*.[147] It is thought therefore that there is reference here to a work of restoration, rather than creation. It is true that καταρτιζω may mean *to reinstate*, but Bagster's *Analytical Greek Lexicon*,[148] Arndt And Gingrich,[149] Abbott-Smith,[150] Thayer,[151] and Vine,[152] are all opposed to rendering it

---

[146] *The Analytical Greek Lexicon,* London, Samuel Bagster, 1870, in.loc.

[147] Custance, op.cit., p. 17.

[148] Op.cit., in.loc.

[149] W. F. Arndt, and F. W. Gingrich, *A Greek-English Lexicon Of The New Testament And Other Early Christian Literature*, Cambridge, the University Press, fourth edition, 1952, in.loc.

[150] G. Abbott-Smith, *A Manual Greek Lexicon Of The New Testament*, Edinburgh, T. & T. Clark, third edition, 1948, in.loc.

in this way in Hebrews 11:3. From the context it is not difficult to see why this is. The whole verse reads:

> "Through faith we understand that the worlds were framed by the Word of God, so that the things which are seen were not made of things which do appear."

Clearly, we see that the subject of this verse is not the restoration of anything, but the tremendous truth that what we see about us, is thoroughly dependent upon the unseen. The Greek word for *made* here is γεγονεναι, a form of γινομαι,[153] the Greek word for *being*.[154] Thus, we do not see here any reference to any kind of a restoration, but, instead a declaration that the visible universe is upheld by, and derives its very being from that which is invisible. It is this theme of the superior quality of that which is unseen over that which is seen, which runs throughout the whole chapter of Hebrews 11, the greatest chapter in Scripture on the nature of faith. The Gap Theorist in his or her eagerness to find a proof text, eliminates the basis of this vital passage in the word of God!

Conclusion 16. Hebrews 11:3 does not refer to a restoration of the world.

II Peter 3:3–6

This text reads in The Authorized Version:

---

[151] *A Greek-English Lexicon Of The New Testament Being Grimm's Wilke's Clovis Novi Testamenti,* translated, revised and enlarged, J. H. Thayer, Grand Rapids, Michigan, U.S.A., 1977, in.loc.

[152] W. E. Vine, *An Expository Dictionary Of New Testament Words,* London, Oliphants, 1975, in.loc.

[153] *The Analytical Greek Lexicon,* op.cit., in.loc.

[154] Ibid., in.loc.

"There shall come in the last days scoffers, walking after their own lusts, and saying, 'Where is the promise of His coming? for since the fathers fell asleep, all things continue as they were from the beginning of the creation.' For this they willingly are ignorant of, that by the word of God the heavens were of old, and the earth standing out of the water and in the water: whereby the world that then was, being overflowed with water, perished."

This reference to the destruction of the world by water is taken not to be a reference to the flood of Noah, but to the ruination of the world by a previous flood, sometimes referred to as Lucifer's Flood, in the supposed gap between Genesis 1:1 and 1:2.

Against this, there are four main points. Firstly, the Flood of Noah is the only Flood explicitly mentioned in the Scriptures; the proposal of any other universal flood is purely speculative. Secondly, Peter had very shortly before this point already referred to the Flood of Noah and the destruction of the world at that time (II Peter 2:5), as he had also in his other epistle (I Peter 3:20). Outside the Gospels there are no other references to the universal Flood, but with Peter, clearly it is a favourite topic. Thirdly, the scoffers Peter mentioned are charged with being *willingly* ignorant of the Flood. This means that these scoffers certainly had had every opportunity of not being ignorant of the Flood Peter refers to, but <u>chose</u> to be ignorant of it. This can only be the case, where information about this Flood is freely available, as is the information concerning Noah's Flood; but this may hardly be said of a supposed Flood before Genesis 1:2, of which Scripture records no details. Finally, the context of the scoffing, is that of disbelief in the Coming of Christ. Now Christ HimSelf likened the days of His Coming again, to the days of Noah's Flood (Matthew 24:36–39, and Luke 17:26–27).

There is then every reason to believe that Peter, like Christ, compared the time of the Second Advent to the time of Noah, and no reason at all to suppose he was referring to some other universal Flood of which Scripture is silent.

Conclusion 17. II Peter 3:3-6 refers to the Flood of Noah.

The Structure of the Apocalypse

The Scriptural comparison between the Second Coming of Christ, and the days of the judgement of the Flood of Noah, has already been referred to. In the Apocalypse, after the coming of the Lord, we encounter the Millennium, during which, the human lifespan appears to resemble very closely, those recorded in Genesis 5 (Revelation 20:1–6). After the Millennium, we see there is a Satanically inspired rebellion, which is then put down, before the creation of a New heaven and earth (Revelation 20:7–22:21). This is held by some Gap Theorists to mirror the alleged Satanic Fall, and ruination of the earth after its creation, and before Genesis 1:2.

The parallelism spoken of here is set out below;

A) The Original Creation of Genesis 1:1.

   B) The alleged gap: the initial Luciferic Rebellion; judgement; the ruination of the old earth.

      C) The antediluvian lifespans of nearly 1,000 years' duration (Genesis 5).

         D) The universal judgement of the Flood of Noah (Genesis 6–8).

         d) The Return of Christ, (compared with the Flood Matthew 24:36–39 and Luke 17:26–27).

      c) The Millennium Reign, during which humans live for 1,000 years (Revelation 20:1-6).

   b) The final rebellion of Satan; judgement; the end of the earth (Revelation 20:7–15).

a) The Creation of the New heavens and earth (Revelation 21–22).

I do believe that there are genuine parallels between Genesis and the Apocalypse, but would point out that the final rebellion of Satan in Revelation 20:7–10 concerns his deceiving the offspring of _Adam_. For this event to mirror any event in the early chapters of Genesis, it must involve this key element of deceiving _humankind_. Only the events associated with the Fall of man comply with this requirement, which means that the counterpart of the Last Rebellion of Satan, and the race of Adam, is the Satanic deception of Eve, and the Fall of Adam (and Eve), in the Garden of Eden. There will be more on this matter in the next Chapter, but for now we must note this aspect clearly. The Gap Theorist must either speculate about an angelic rebellion, led by Lucifer within the alleged gap, or, he must speak in terms of pre-Adamites. Either way, _the link with Adam is broken, and the parallelism with the final rebellion of the race of Adam in Revelation 20 is shattered_. Thus, a proper consideration of the parallels between Genesis and the Apocalypse excludes the concept of a gap between Genesis 1:1 and 1:2, but unites the first rebellion of Satan with Adam.

Conclusion 18. The parallels between Genesis and the Apocalypse do not support the Gap Theory.

Conclusion 19. The parallels between Genesis and the Apocalypse connect the first rebellion of Satan with Adam.

Summary

None of the texts listed above gives any support for the Gap Theory, and the considerations of the phrase _the foundation of the world_, actually tends to undermine the theory.

Part Three

The Consequences

Chapter Five

The consequences of the gap theory

We have seen from a detailed analysis of the text of Genesis 1:1–2, that not only is there no evidence for the Gap Theory in these verses, but that contrariwise, they present the strongest evidence imaginable *against* the Gap Theory. We have also found that these findings derived from what might be called the Primary Evidence, are substantiated fully by what might be termed the Secondary Evidence, namely, texts found throughout the Hebrew and Christian Scriptures, which it is alleged, provide support for the Gap Theory. The conclusion must be then, that the Gap Theory is untenable and is to be rejected.

But now the question of the importance of the Gap Theory presents itself. The theory does not affect directly our conception of the Persons of the Godhead, although the less common variant which places the gap before Genesis 1:1 removes a potent argument for the transcendence of God as we have seen. Nor does it affect our understanding of soteriology, ecclesiology, anthropology, or eschatology. It does however, affect our understanding of the Luciferic Fall, and the place of man in that tragedy, and it is in this, I believe that the importance of the controversy lies.

Were the Gap Theory to be true, the Fall of Lucifer would necessarily and inevitably predate the creation of Adam by an unspecified expanse of time, and, therefore, the two events would be absolutely unrelated. Rejection of the Gap Theory however, inevitably drives these two events into the closest proximity, which helps our understanding of them greatly.

When we consider the events of the hexameron, we notice that there is something different about the creation of man. With the creation of plant life, the heavenly bodies, winged life, marine life, and also with the creation of wild and domestic terrestrial life, we are left with the impression that whole *multitudes* of creatures were created simultaneously (Genesis 1:20, "Let the waters bring forth *abundantly*.") Against this background of teeming multiplicity, the uniqueness, solitariness, and individuality of man stands out starkly; *he is the only one of his kind.* Reflecting the uniqueness of His Maker, the One God, amidst the multiplicity of life forms surrounding him, the potential woman still within him, man as a conspicuous and significant unity stands alone.

In the very image of the One God, and bearing His likeness, he was to have dominion over all the other life forms that roamed around him. In his essential nature, he is like God, though he is formed from the mere dust of the ground. Now from the book of Job, we know that the Sons of God, among whom was Lucifer, later, Satan (Job 1:6), watched with awe and excitement, the bringing forth of the dry land from the waters (Job 38:1–7). We may be certain then that the creation of man, and the special nature of that event, were observed keenly by the angelic hosts.

Yet, given that there is no gap before Genesis 1:1, or between Genesis 1:1 and 1:2, the declaration by God in Genesis 1:31 on the sixth day that everything that He had made "was very good" must include the angelic hosts as well, for the word *everything*, must include just that, whether Genesis 1 informs us about it or not. Therefore Lucifer was unfallen when Adam was created; God's creation in its entirety was unmarred in its perfection. By contrast, the Gap Theory of course makes Lucifer a fallen being way before the hexameron, leading to a qualification, or restriction, being imposed upon God's declaration of Genesis 1:31, for then, in spite of these words, evil was present.

The Sons of God no doubt watched as YHWH Elohim breathed the breath of lives into Adam, instructed him personally, and caused the animals to come to him for naming. It would have been obvious to these Sons of God, that Adam was of the highest significance. When the Deep Sleep fell upon him, and the woman was formed from his side, and the void filled up with flesh, the headship of Adam received its final and emphatic confirmation, and, I propose, the jealousy of Lucifer awoke. We notice from Isaiah, the sinful ambition in Lucifer's cry, "I will be *like* the Most High" (Isaiah 14:14). The likeness of God that pertained to Adam, was noted and coveted by Lucifer, in his jealousy of Adam's rôle. We perhaps notice also in the temptation of Eve, a subtle denial by the serpent, of the truth that man was created in the likeness of God, inasmuch as the prospect of being as God was presented as a goal to be achieved by human endeavour through the acquisition of knowledge, rather than by simply accepting it as the gift of God (Genesis 3:5). The implication might have been, that they were *not* made in the likeness of God, a state Satan desired for himself, and, therefore would be likely to refuse to recognise within man.

Thus, we see that rejection of the Gap theory inevitably forces together the Fall of Lucifer, ambitious to be like God, and the creation of the image and likeness of God within Adam. How galling to Satan that when the Logos became manifest in flesh, as Jesus Christ, it was as a man; as a Second Adam; how bitter the defeat when salvation was wrought through the death of this Second Adam, when he himself had triumphed by bringing death to the first Adam! How vexing for him to consider:

> "That in the dispensation of the fulness of times
> He (God) might gather together in one all things
> in Christ, both which are in heaven, and which
> are on earth" (Ephesians 1:10),

so that, within Christ, man will achieve an even greater dominion than was promised to Adam. We know that by the uniting of the redeemed within Christ, God's wisdom is even now being revealed to the unseen realms, which would include the fallen angels (Ephesians 3:10–11).

This enables us to understand more keenly Satan's hatred for mankind, and his peculiar hatred of Christ. His Fall is bound up with the creation of man and his insane jealousy of his position. The history of man's redemption, and the exaltation of him, to a situation greater than any finite mind can comprehend, would but cause that hatred to resort to acts of the greatest depravity, in the pitiless pursuit of revenge, driven by a rage and madness the depths of which we will never know.

Believers will benefit from seeing that the creation of their first human father is what provoked the jealousy of Lucifer, and led to his Fall, and from understanding that to his jealousy for us, a diabolical hatred has been added. Further, by the propagation of the Gap Theory I believe the evil one also seeks to create the false-impression that he has achieved an independence from the Creator which might be seen as *viable*, inasmuch as it would be thought of as having endured for very many millennia, even perhaps for many millions of years.

So as not to leave this study in an unbalanced condition, we ought also to recognize the truth that we should rejoice in the fact that by being born from *Above* (John 3:3–6), we derive our new nature from a realm beyond the reach of Satan, and that while we walk this earth, simultaneously, we are at God's right hand, in Christ (Ephesians 2:5–7, Colossians 3:1–4), Who as the Second and Triumphant Adam, has defeated the evil one finally, and irreversibly, and thereby has made absolutely certain the ending of the evil one's foolish and short-lived rebellion. We must not allow the untenable Gap Theory to rob us of these insights, especially that which shows that the Luciferic Fall was induced by jealousy over the nature and destiny of man.

Part Four

Appendices and Bibliography

Appendix I

Use of רֵאשִׁית

Every instance of רֵאשִׁית in the Hebrew Canon is listed below.[155] Those in italics and underlined, are where רֵאשִׁית is an Absolute; those in bold and underlined, are the instances of בְּרֵאשִׁית. The renderings of רֵאשִׁית in the Authorized Version are in underlined upper-case.

Reference	How used
Genesis 1:1	**IN THE BEGINNING God created the heavens and the earth.**
Genesis 10:10	And THE BEGINNING of his Kingdom was Babel.
Genesis 49:3	Reuben, thou are my firstborn, my might, AND THE BEGINNING of my strength.
Exodus 23:19	THE FIRST of the First-fruits.
Exodus 34:26	THE FIRST of the First-fruits.
Leviticus 2:12	*As for the oblation of THE FIRST FRUITS.*
Leviticus 23:10	Ye shall bring a sheaf of THE FIRST FRUITS of your harvest.
Numbers 15:20	Ye shall offer up a cake of THE FIRST of your dough.
Numbers 15:21	OF THE FIRST of your dough ye shall give unto the Lord.

---

[155] Based on Wigram, op.cit., in.loc.

Reference	How used
Numbers 18:12	All the best of the oil, and all the best of the wine, and of the wheat, THE FIRST FRUITS of them which they shall offer unto the Lord.
Numbers 24:20	Amalek was THE FIRST of the nations.
Deuteronomy 11:12	FROM THE BEGINNING of the year even unto the end of the year.
Deuteronomy 18:4a	THE FIRSTFRUITS also of thy corn, of thy wine, and of thine oil.
Deuteronomy 18:4b	AND THE FIRST of the fleece of thy sheep.
Deuteronomy 21:17	He is THE BEGINNING of his strength; the right of the firstborn is his.
Deuteronomy 26:2	Thou shalt take OF THE FIRST of all the fruits of the earth.
Deuteronomy 26:10	I have brought THE FIRSTFRUITS of the land.
Deuteronomy 33:21	*And he provided THE FIRST PART for himself.*
I Samuel 2:29	The CHIEFEST of all the offerings.
I Samuel 15:21	THE CHIEF of the things which should have been utterly destroyed.
II Chronicles 31:5	THE FIRST FRUITS of corn, wine and oil.
Nehemiah 10:37	THE FIRST FRUITS of our dough.
Nehemiah 12:44	*For the offerings, FOR THE FIRST FRUITS, and for the tithes.*
Job 8:7	And though THY BEGINNING was small, yet thy latter end should greatly increase.
Job 40:19	He is THE CHIEF of the ways of God.
Job 42:12	So the Lord blessed the latter end of Job MORE THAN HIS BEGINNING.

Reference	How used
Psalms 78:51	And smote all the Firstborn in Egypt; THE CHIEF of their strength.
Psalms 105:36	He smote also all the Firstborn of their land, THE CHIEF of all their strength.
Psalms 111:10	The fear of the Lord is THE BEGINNING of wisdom.
Proverbs 1:7	The fear of the Lord is THE BEGINNING of knowledge.
Proverbs 3:9	Honour the Lord with thy substance, WITH THE FIRST FRUITS of all thine increase.
Proverbs 4:7	*Wisdom is THE PRINCIPAL THING.*
Proverbs 8:22	The Lord possessed Me in THE BEGINNING of His way.
Proverbs 17:14	THE BEGINNING of strife.
Ecclesiastes 7:8	Better is the end of a thing THAN THE BEGINNING thereof.
Isaiah 46:10	*Declaring the end FROM THE BEGINNING.*
Jeremiah 2:3	Israel was Holiness-Unto-The-Lord, and THE FIRST FRUITS of His increase.
Jeremiah 26:1	**IN THE BEGINNING of the reign of Jehoiakim.**
Jeremiah 27:1	**IN THE BEGINNING of the reign of Jehoiakim.**
Jeremiah 28:1	**IN THE BEGINNING of the reign of Zedekiah.**
Jeremiah 49:34	**IN THE BEGINNING of the reign of Zedekiah.**

Reference	How used
Jeremiah 49:35	Behold, I will break the bow of Elam, <u>THE CHIEF</u> of their might.
Ezekiel 20:40	I require your offerings, <u>AND THE FIRST FRUITS</u> of your oblations.
Ezekiel 44:30a	<u>AND THE FIRST</u> of all the First Fruits.
Ezekiel 44:30b	<u>THE FIRST</u> of your dough.
Ezekiel 48:14	<u>THE FIRST FRUITS</u> of the land.
Daniel 11:41	<u>AND THE CHIEF</u> of the children of Ammon.
Hosea 9:10	**I saw your fathers as the firstripe in the fig tree <u>AT HER FIRST TIME</u>.**
Amos 6:1	<u>CHIEF</u> of the nations.
Amos 6:6	<u>THE CHIEF</u> ointments.
Micah 1:13	<u>THE BEGINNING</u> of sin.

Appendix II

Use of תחלה

Every instance of תחלה in the Hebrew Canon is listed below.[156] The renderings of תחלה in the Authorized Version are in underlined upper-case.

Reference	How Used
Genesis 13:3	His tent had been AT THE BEGINNING.
Genesis 41:21	Ill favoured, as AT THE BEGINNING.
Genesis 43:18	In our sacks AT THE FIRST TIME.
Genesis 43:20	Down AT THE FIRST TIME.
Judges 1:1	Go up for us against the Canaanites FIRST.
Judges 20:18a	Which of us shall go up FIRST.
Judges 20:18b	Judah shall go up FIRST.
Ruth 1:22	IN THE BEGINNING OF barley harvest.
II Samuel 17:9	Overthrown AT THE FIRST.
II Samuel 21:9	IN THE BEGINNING OF barley harvest.
II Samuel 21:10	FROM THE BEGINNING OF harvest.
II Kings 17:25	AT THE BEGINNING OF their dwelling.
Ezra 4:6	In the reign of Ahasuerus, IN THE BEGINNING OF his reign.
Nehemiah 11:17	To BEGIN the thanksgiving.

---

[156] Based on Wigram, op.cit., in.loc.

Reference	How Used
Proverbs 9:10	The fear of the Lord is THE BEGINNING OF wisdom.
Ecclesiastes 10:13	THE BEGINNINGS OF the words.
Isaiah 1:26	Counsellors AS AT THE BEGINNING.
Daniel 8:1	Appeared unto me AT THE FIRST.
Daniel 9:21	Had seen in the vision AT THE BEGINNING.
Daniel 9:23	AT THE BEGINNING OF thy supplications.
Hosea 1:	THE BEGINNING OF the Word of the Lord.
Amos 7:1	Grasshoppers IN THE BEGINNING OF.

Appendix III

Occurrences of תהו and use of בהו

I list below and categorise every occurrence of תהו. This analysis also reveals every usage of בהו, as בהו is only found on three occasions, and on each it is associated with תהו. These three occasions are given in bold, and are underlined.

Reference	Used to describe
Genesis 1:2	The emptiness of an unpopulated expanse.
Deuteronomy 32:10	The emptiness of an unpopulated expanse.
I Samuel 12:21a	The emptiness of whatever replaces the Lord in peoples' hearts.
I Samuel 12:21b	The emptiness of whatever replaces the Lord in peoples' hearts.
Job 6:18	The emptiness of the bed of a dried up river.
Job 12:24	The emptiness of an unpopulated expanse.
Job 26:7	The emptiness of an unpopulated expanse.
Psalms 107:40	The emptiness of an unpopulated expanse.
Isaiah 24:10	The moral vacuum of a cultural centre opposed to God's ways.
Isaiah 29:21	That which is void of any value.
Isaiah 34:11	The emptiness of an unpopulated expanse.
Isaiah 40:17	The inconsequential size of nations compared with the Infinite God.
Isaiah 40:23	The lowly state human dignitaries may be brought to by the Lord.

Reference	Used to describe
Isaiah 41:29	The emptiness of idolatry.
Isaiah 44:9	The emptiness of idolatry.
Isaiah 45:18	The emptiness of futile activity.
Isaiah 45:19	The emptiness of futile activity.
Isaiah 49:4	The emptiness of futile activity.
Isaiah 59:4	The emptiness of godlessness.
Jeremiah 4:23	The emptiness of an unpopulated expanse.

We see that the meanings range from that of a literal waste or desert, to the metaphorical wasteland of idolatry and godlessness. While godlessness and idolatry undoubtedly are evils, the thought conveyed by the Hebrew words under consideration is not that of wickedness itself, but rather that of the *emptiness* or *futility* of godlessness. The conclusion must be then that תהו ובהו refers to the concept of literal or moral barrenness.

Appendix IV

Occurrences of ברא and עשה within the first creation account

In the table below I list every occurrence of ברא and עשה within the first account of the Creation (Genesis 1:1–2:4). The table shows the sequence of these occurrences, and reveals those verses where both words are found.

ברא	עשה
Genesis 1:1.	
	Genesis 1:7.
	Genesis 1:11.
	Genesis 1:12.
	Genesis 1:16.
Genesis 1:21.	
	Genesis 1:25.
	Genesis 1:26.
Genesis 1:27a.	
Genesis 1:27b.	
Genesis 1:27c.	
	Genesis 1:31.
	Genesis 2:2a.
	Genesis 2:2b.
Genesis 2:3.	Genesis 2:3.
Genesis 2:4.	Genesis 2:4.

Bibliography

Texts and Versions

Concordant Version Of The Old Testament: The Book Of "Genesis": In A Beginning, Canyon Country, California, Concordant Publishing Concern, 1978.

Good News Bible: Today's English Version, London, Collins/Fontana, 1973.

Tanakh: A New Translation Of The Holy Scriptures According To The Traditional Hebrew Text, Philadelphia, U.S.A., The Jewish Publication Society, 1985.

The Authorized King James Version, Oxford, The University Press, undated.

The Bible In Basic English, Cambridge, The University Press, 1965.

The Companion Bible, London, The Lamp Press, undated.

The Holy Bible Translated From The Latin Vulgate And Diligently Compared With The Hebrew, Greek, And Other Editions In Divers Languages, London, Burns & Oates, undated.

The Holy Bible With Twenty Thousand Emendations, London, Longman, Brown & Co., 1843.

The Holy Bible: A Translation From The Latin Vulgate In The Light Of The Hebrew And The Greek Originals, translated Knox, London, Burns & Oates, 1963.

The Holy Bible: American Standard Version, Nashville, U.S.A., Thomas Nelson, 1929.

The Holy Bible: New International Version, London, Hodder & Stoughton, 1979.

The Holy Bible: Revised Standard Version, London, Collins, 1971.

The Holy Bible: Revised Version, Oxford, The University Press, 1928.

The Jewish Study Bible, edited Berlin, Adele, Brettler, Marc Zvi., & Fishbane, Michael, Oxford, Oxford University Press, 2004.

The Living Bible: Paraphrased, Minneapolis, U.S.A., World Wide Publications, 1971.

The New English Bible, Oxford, The University Press, 1970.

The New Testament In Hebrew And English, Edgware, Middlesex, The Society For Distributing The Holy Scriptures To The Jews, undated.

The Sacred Scriptures: Concordant Literal New Testament, Canyon County, California, Concordant Publishing Concern, sixth edition, 1976.

The Septuagint With Apocrypha: Greek And English, translated Brenton, Sir Lancelot C. L., Peabody, Massachusetts, U.S.A., Hendrickson, 1997.

ספרי הברית החדשה Jerusalem, The United Bible Societies, 1979.

Bowes, (translator). *The New Testament Translated From The Purest Greek*, Dundee, published privately by the author, 1870.

Darby, J. N. (translator). *The 'Holy Scriptures': A New Translation From The Original Languages*, London, Stow Hill Bible And Tract Depot, 1946.

Ferrar Fenton, (translator). *The Holy Bible In Modern English*, London, A. & C. Black, 1938.

Green, Jay P., Sr. (Editor & translator). *The Interlinear Bible: Hebrew-Greek-English*, Peabody, Massachusetts, U.S.A., Hendrickson, 1985.

Knoch, A. E., (translator). *The Concordant Version: The Sacred Scriptures*, translated Knoch, A. E., Los Angeles, California, The Concordant Publishing Concern, revised edition, 1930.

Moffatt, J. (translator). *A New Translation Of The Bible*, London, Hodder & Stoughton, Revised Edition, 1934.

Rotherham, J. B., (translator). *The Emphasised Bible: A New Translation*, Cincinnati, U.S.A., Four Volumes, The Standard Publishing Company, 1916.

Scofield, & Schuyler, (editors). *The New Scofield Reference Bible*, Oxford, The University Press, 1967.

Young, Robert, (translator). *Literal Translation Of The Holy Bible*, Grand Rapids, Michigan, U.S.A., Baker Books, 2000.

General

The Analytical Greek Lexicon, London, Samuel Bagster, 1870.

The Hebrew Student's Manual, London, Samuel Bagster, undated.

Abbott-Smith, A.   *A Manual Greek Lexicon Of The New Testament*, Edinburgh, T. & T. Clark, third edition, 1948.

Arndt, W. F., & Gingrich, F. W.   *A Greek-English Lexicon Of The New Testament And Other Early Christian Literature*, Cambridge, The University Press, fourth edition, 1952.

Augustine of Hippo.   *The City Of God*, translated Bettenson, Harmondsworth, Penguin Books, 1977.

Boman, Thorleif.   *Hebrew Thought Compared With Greek*, London, SCM Press, undated.

Bullinger, E. W.,   *The Apocalypse Or "The Day Of The Lord,"* London, Eyre & Spottiswoode, 1935.

Custance, Arthur C.   *Without Form And Void*, Brookville, Canada, published privately by the author, 1970.

Davidson, Benjamin.   *The Analytical Hebrew And Chaldee Lexicon*, Grand Rapids Michigan, U.S.A., Zondervan, undated.

Davies, Benjamin.   *A Compendious And Complete Hebrew And Chaldee Lexicon To The Old Testament*, London, Asher & Co., 1889.

Driver, S. R.   *The Book Of Genesis*, London, Methuen & Co., 1905.

124

Fields, Weston, W.   *Unformed And Unfilled: A Critique Of The Gap Theory*, Collinsville, Illinois, U.S.A., Burgener Enterprises, undated.

Frey, J. S. C. F.   *A Hebrew Grammar In The English Language*, London, Henry G. Bohn, 1859.

Gesenius, H. W. F.   *Hebrew And Chaldee Lexicon Of The Old Testament Scriptures*, translated Tregelles, S. P., Grand Rapids, Michigan, U.S.A., Baker Book House, 1984.

Gesenius, H. W. F.   *Hebrew Grammar*, edited and enlarged Kautzsch, translated Cowley, Oxford, The University Press, second edition from the corrected sheets, 1966.

Green, Samuel.   *A Handbook Of Old Testament Hebrew*, London, The Religious Tract Society, 1901.

Hatch, E., & Redpath, H. A.   *A Concordance To The Septuagint*, Grand Rapids, Michigan, U.S.A., Baker Books, 1998.

Hooker, J. T.   *Reading The Past*, London, British Museum Publications, 1990.

Keil, C. F. & Delitzsch, F.   *Commentary On The Old Testament*, Volume I., Grand Rapids, Michigan, U.S.A., Ten Volumes, Eerdmans, 1978.

Kelly, Page H.   *Biblical Hebrew: An Introductory Grammar*, Grand Rapids, Michigan, Eerdmans, 1992.

Kelley, P. H., Mynatt, D. S., & Crawford, T. G.   *The Masorah Of Biblia Hebraica Stutgartensia*, Grand Rapids, Michigan, U.S.A., Eerdmans, 1998.

Knight, George A. F.   *A Christian Theology Of The Old Testament*, London, SCM Press, revised edition, 1964.

Liddell & Scott,   *Greek-English Lexicon*, Oxford, The University Press, undated.

Parkhurst, John.   *An Hebrew And Chaldee Lexicon Without Points*, London, 1813.

Parrot, A.   *The Flood And Noah's Ark*, translated Hudson, London, SCM Press, 1955.

Pember, G. H.   *Earth's Earliest Ages*, London, Pickering & Inglis, undated.

Phelan, M. W. J.   *The Inspiration Of The Pentateuch*, Waterlooville, Twoedged Sword Publications, 2005.

Roddy, A. J.   *Exegesis Of Genesis 1:1–2*, being an article in Scripture Research, Volume II, Number 16, Atascadero, California, Ewalt Memorial School Incorporated, undated.

Sarna, N. H.   *The JPS Torah Commentary: Genesis*, Philadelphia, U.S.A., The Jewish Publication Society, 5749 (1989).

Sayce, A. H.   *Monument Facts, And Higher Critical Fancies*, London, The Religious Tract Society, 1904.

Sayce, A. H.   *The "Higher Criticism" And The Verdict Of The Monuments*, London, The Society For Promoting Christian Knowledge, 1915.

Schaefer, R. H.   *Before The Foundation Of The World*, being an article in Scripture Research, Volume II, Number 16, Atascadero, California, Ewalt Memorial School Incorporated, undated.

Snaith, Norman, H.   *Notes On The Hebrew Text Of Genesis I–VIII*, London, The Epworth Press, 1947.

Steele-Smith, W. E.   *Wonders Of The Hebrew Alphabet*, Sydney, The Central Press, undated.

Stern, D.   *The Jewish New Testament Commentary*, Clarksville, Maryland, U.S.A., Jewish New Testament Publications, sixth edition, 1999.

126

Strong, A. H.   *Systematic Theology: A Compendium Designed For The Use Of Theological Students*, London, Pickering & Inglis, 1981.

Thayer, J. H.   *A Greek-English Lexicon Of The New Testament Being Grimm's Wilke's Clovis Novi Testamenti*, translated, revised and enlarged, Thayer, Grand Rapids, Michigan, U.S.A., Baker Book House, 1977.

Tilney, A. G.   *Redefinitions Of Biblical Terms And Phrases*, Hayling Island, published privately by the author, undated.

Vine, W. E.   *An Expository Dictionary Of New Testament Words*, London, Oliphants, 1975.

Whitcomb, J. C. Jr.   *The Early Earth*, London, Evangelical Press, 1972.

Wigram, George, V.   *The Englishman's Hebrew And Chaldee Concordance Of The Old Testament*, Grand Rapids, Michigan, U.S.A., Zondervan, 1970.

Wiseman, P. J.   *New Discoveries In Babylonia About Genesis*, London, Marshall, Morgan & Scott, seventh edition, 1958.

Young, Edward J.   *Studies In Genesis One*, Philadelphia, U.S.A., Presbyterian And Reformed, 1964.

Young, Robert.   *Concise Critical Comments On The Holy Bible*, London, Pickering & Inglis, undated.

**Other books by M. W. J. Phelan published by
Twoedged Sword Publications**

The Christology of Philippians 2:6–11
An examination of the Person and Work of Christ

M. W. J. Phelan, B.Th., M.Th., Th.D.

ISBN 0-9547205-1-2

By accepting that all the Scriptures centre on Christ; that all the believer's hopes centre upon Him; and that we are acceptable to God only through Him and His Work, all true believers practice Christology. This book exposes the so-called Kenotic Theology as a falsehood. This doctrine teaches that the Deity of Christ was compromised when He took our flesh. The danger of this doctrine is made worse by the fact that it may seem to be correct, but, as this book reveals, it is based upon a fundamental misunderstanding. Many believers will find this book to be of real interest and benefit, especially as it could easily be used as the basis for a small study group, in which believers may explore together the exhilarating truths dealt with by the writer.

The Inspiration of the Pentateuch
or
The Graf-Wellhausen Fallacy

An examination of the origins of the Torah, the inadequacies and contradictions of cynical Source Criticism, and the merits of Faithful Source, and Form Criticism.

M. W. J. Phelan, B.Th., M.Th., Th.D., Ph.D.

ISBN 0-9547205-6-3

Christianity claims the Bible is a comprehensive collection of truths concerning the nature and purposes of God, and the nature and destiny of mankind. It claims that this Divinely Inspired, and therefore, utterly inerrant revelation was transmitted to us through the New Testament. However, this collection of documents rests upon the Hebrew Canon, or Old Testament, and the very foundation of the Hebrew Canon, is the Torah, or Pentateuch, or Five-Books-Of-Moses; namely, Genesis, Exodus, Leviticus, Numbers, and Deuteronomy. It is the Pentateuch that has been the target of the most unremitting assaults of sceptics and critics down the years, and the Book of Genesis has suffered the most brutal of these attacks. It is these assaults upon the Pentateuch that form the subject of this book.

The Integrity of Isaiah: New evidence of single authorship

A practical demonstration of the literary unity of the book of Isaiah

M. W. J. Phelan, B.Th., M.Th., Th.D., Ph.D.

ISBN 1-905447-03-5

For over two thousand years the book of Isaiah was accepted as the exclusive work of the son of Amoz, the friend of Hezekiah. The translators of the Septuagint regarded the book as a single work. The well-known discovery at Qumran in 1947 of two different copies of Isaiah also testifies to its unity. One of these scrolls is virtually complete and is normally dated to the late second century B.C.E.

The New Testament adds its very considerable, and for the believer, decisive weight to the traditional viewpoint, as may be seen from the eighty-seven occasions where it cites the prophet's words. In no less than twenty-one of these instances, the quotation from the book is accompanied by a reference to the prophet Isaiah by name.

In addition to this, the Masoretic Text, the standard Hebrew text of the Hebrew Canon, and the unanimous testimony of all the ancient texts, versions, Jewish traditions, and the early Christian Church, report the book to be a single work.

At the end of the eighteenth century however, this view that had held sway for millennia began to be challenged. Isaiah, it was asserted was a compilation by different authors, and various so-called proofs of this were brought forth by the critics. Since then, this view-point has gained a massive momentum so that it is now considered to be the orthodox scholarly position. We are assured that critical scholarship has demonstrated the separate existence of the work of no less than three authors, usually referred to as Proto-Isaiah, Deutero-Isaiah, and Trito-Isaiah.

The issues raised by this challenge to the traditional belief, are firstly and obviously, that the Hebrew Canon is charged with containing pseudonymous works, but secondly, and more importantly, the authority of the New Testament is gravely undermined, as the twenty-one occasions where Isaiah is referred to by name, relate to every section of the book, and, therefore, to all three of the modernist's authors.

Either the evangelists and Paul were unaware of what has supposedly been unearthed by the critics, and thereby face the charge of gross ignorance; or they were not ignorant at all, but accommodated themselves to the prejudices of those they wrote for, and, thereby, knowingly and deliberately maintained a falsehood. For believers then, the matter is not merely of academic interest, but affects his or her faith in the Inspiration of the New Testament. A New Testament that through ignorance or deliberate policy propagates and maintains a falsehood cannot be Divinely Inspired, or relied upon as our guide in the most vital issues which confront us all, the issues of life and death in their eternal dimensions. Clearly then the matter must be resolved, and either the New Testament, or the views of the critics must be abandoned; the matter is as stark as that.

Other books published by Twoedged Sword Publications

Try the spirits: volume 1

Cecil Andrews

ISBN 0-9547205-2-0

- Was C S Lewis truly 'Our greatest Christian writer'?

- Philip Yancey—'turning the grace of God into lasciviousness'?

- Alpha—Attend or Avoid?

When the writer first formed 'Take Heed' Ministries some fourteen years ago most of the warnings issued on spiritual deception would have referred to matters outside of professing Christendom. Today the spiritual make-up of that professing Christendom is both very different and very dangerous. There has been a biblically-predicted (1 Timothy 4:1 and 2 Timothy 4:3) marked decline in discernment amongst professing Christians and the result is that the questionable views of certain apologists, authors and advocates, who are viewed by many as Christian, have increased dramatically both in popularity and influence. This book is an attempt to bring biblical truth to bear on three such current dangers that are deceiving many.

Try the spirits: volume 2

Cecil Andrews

ISBN 0-9547205-5-5

- Catholic Catechism—some non-Christian teachings
- 'Father' McCafferty—Catholic but not Christian
- Alister McGrath—misrepresenting the Catholic Catechism?
- ECT Ireland—the myth of Evangelicals and Catholics Together in Ireland
- Evangelising Roman Catholics

Almost five hundred years ago the Roman Catholic domination of professing Christendom was broken as God, by His Spirit, moved in the hearts, minds and understanding of many who had found no peace with God through their adherence to, and reliance upon, priestly Roman Catholic ritual. The rediscovery of the great biblical truth of 'justification through faith alone in Christ alone' became central to what is known as The Reformation. Today, many appear to have forgotten the spiritual lessons of that crucial period and for a number of decades now Romanism has once more been rising to a position of dominance like the proverbial Phoenix from the ashes. This bodes ill for the eternal well-being of countless souls. May the One who alone has saved His people from their sins be pleased to use this little volume to counter the claims of a false anti-Christian system that is so loved by the world today.

Condemned, Condoned or Confused?
The Contemporary World in the Light of God's Word

Timothy Cross, BA (Hons), BD (Hons), Th.D.

ISBN 0-9547205-3-9

- Bad language
- The cult of the celebrity
- The family
- The status and role of women
- Homosexuality
- Gambling
- Alcohol

This book considers these, and many other prominent aspects of our modern world, in the light of God's Word—which is the correct standard by which to *prove all things* (1 Thessalonians 5:21). Sadly, when our contemporary society is tested in the light of God's unchanging Word it is often *weighed in the balances, and... found wanting* (Daniel 5:27). But the situation is not hopeless, for the Bible shows us where we have strayed from God's way and how we can return to God's way, the only way to true happiness, peace and eternal life. Only the Bible can make us truly wise, as only the Bible can impart the wisdom of God.

Some Postcards from John:
2 and 3 John for today

Timothy Cross, BA (Hons), BD (Hons), Th.D.

ISBN 0-9547205-7-1

The 'postcards' that John wrote to the churches of 2 and 3 John are packed full of useful instruction and exhortation. John sent these 'postcards' on ahead of hoped for, and longed for face to face visits: in 2 John to *the elect lady and her children* and in 3 John to *the beloved Gaius*.

Both churches had their problems. The problem in the church of 2 John concerned deceiving deviants from outside the church—*men who will not acknowledge the coming of Jesus Christ in the flesh*, whilst the problem addressed in 3 John was concerned mainly with a dreadful dictator from within the church—*Diotrephes, who likes to put himself first, does not acknowledge my authority*. These problem personalities from the first century will ring many present-day bells with us in the twenty-first century.

In John's 'postcards', we encounter doctrine, duty, affirmation of truth, and warning against error. We meet love and discipline along with affection and sternness. Overriding everything, as everywhere in the Bible, we glimpse something of the supernatural glory of God in contrast with the sinful humanity He sent His Own Son to save.

At the end of each chapter there is a set of thought-provoking and stimulating questions, each of which could be the subject of a Bible study group.

An Exposition of I Peter Chapter I

Robert A. Penney B.D., D.Min.

ISBN 0-9547205-4-7

The lessons that Peter brings to us might have been written with our current times in mind, such is the relevance and agelessness of Scripture. In expounding these great truths, the author considers the following subjects:

- Apostleship
- Election
- Worship, Mercy and Lively Hope
- The Preservation of the believer
- Heaviness
- The Trial of Faith
- Unseen but Loved
- The Desire of Prophets
- The Desire of Angels
- Holiness
- Redeemed by Blood
- The Christian's Hope and Faith in God's Power
- The Transient Nature of our Existence and the Eternal Nature of the Word of God
- Vain Glory: The Enduring Word

An Exposition of II Peter chapter 3

Robert A. Penney B.D., D.Min.

ISBN 0-9547205-9-8

The old adage says: "Your bible is more up-to-date than your morning's newspaper." Such a statement was never more true than when applied to this third chapter of Peter's second epistle. It has to do with the present state of affairs and gives us a brief insight into the end time and also a glimpse of the nature of the future kingdom. To live amid this present godless world with such Scriptures saturating our minds and our souls is richness indeed and fills the believer with hope, confidence and faith in these modern times of unbelief and apostasy.

These addresses are sent forth trusting that the result will be the strengthening of all who read them, that hope may be instilled within those who may be discouraged in these wicked times and that even thrill and excitement may be aroused as one contemplates the believer's lot in this present evil world and the glories which will follow. Nothing is more needful today than for the Christian to be encouraged in the things he has most surely believed.

The author has written this small book to encourage Christians to rejoice in the hope of their high calling and to consider the eventual triumph of Christ and His Church over Satan and his forces and over the ungodliness of men which is so characteristic of these last days. But the chapter under consideration is also full of warnings for the believer—the appearance of evil on an unprecedented scale, the ultimate wrath of God in judgment upon it all and how we must get back to spiritual basics by heeding the teaching of the apostles and prophets.

A Faith for the Times

Robert A. Penney B.D., D.Min.

ISBN 0-9547205-8-X

Only One Message • Liberty in the Spirit • The Power of the Spirit • The Demonstration of the Spirit • The Power of God • Impossibilities • Divine Revelation • Divine Commission • Departed Glory • The Flickering Lamp • Leadership • The Function of the Local Church • Treasures of Darkness • Fire! • Scotland's Finest Hour • Righteousness

Dr Robert A. Penney addresses the problems of a people that has turned its back on God: materialism, moral depravity, humanism, philosophy, sin in high places. He reflects on the ways in which God dealt with the people of Israel and its leaders, the early New Testament Church as well as some of the problems in the modern Church.

'When you read the Bible and get to know it thoroughly, you will find that it is a book that speaks to every age and generation, because mankind remains the same in all its essential qualities, and God remains the same.'—Dr. Martyn Lloyd-Jones

Dr Penney spent over twenty years as a Probation Officer in the Birmingham courts. On early retirement he studied at the Scottish Congregational College and New College, Edinburgh, whilst serving as an assistant to the late Dr Nelson Gray at Portobello Congregational Church. He pastored Beith Congregational Church, Ayrshire, for a short period before resigning to devote himself to writing and itinerant ministry. He now lives in Kirkintilloch, his home town, near Glasgow.

***Things which must shortly come to pass: a study of
Revelation***

Paul Rose

ISBN 0-9547205-0-4

The things John wrote in the book of Revelation were revealed
to him by the Lord Jesus Christ Himself. They are *things
which must shortly come to pass* (Revelation 1:1). Many
Revelation prophesies have already been fulfilled and those
who keep an eye on the political arena can see the way being
prepared for the fulfilment of more Revelation prophecies. In
the writer's opinion we should study Revelation with renewed
enthusiasm because *these things must shortly come to pass.*

Angels Everwatching

Robert Baghurst, Rosemarie Baghurst, Timothy Baghurst, Amy Baghurst

ISBN 1-905447-00-0

"Liberia's motto has always intrigued me... 'For the Love of Liberty brought us here.' It has always been their boast to be the first African nation that was free, all the others having first been colonised. Actually this has been to their disadvantage since they had no strong Western influence to educate, support, and give them a good basis from which to work and grow. To the contrary, they have always been a poor nation, proud to be free, but wholly enslaved to the animistic traditions which they tenaciously hold."

The Liberian civil war erupted in December 1989, when the National Patriotic Front of Liberia (NPFL), a military force led by Charles Ghankay Taylor, a former official of the Liberian government, invaded Liberia from the Ivory Coast. He received the assistance of mercenaries from other nations, with many recruits from the Mano and Gio ethnic groups. The Baghurst family found themselves in the path of this force and for a time found themselves captives. During their experience they learned that the "angel of the LORD encampeth round about them that fear him, and delivereth them" (Psalm 34:7). This is that story.